Advance Praise for

PRIVATE NOTES OF A HEADHUNTER

"The book announces the very serious rite of passage facing today's college graduate. Uniquely and magnificently it contains the Dark Side of the interview process: all the variables and agendas the job seeker may be totally unaware of in the corporate culture, both the institution and the individual across the table. The tone of the book is intimate, feels like a personal relationship and conversation with the reader ... as though a friendly uncle who has been through the wars has shown up to save my ass as I head off to corporate no-man's-land."

     — Brenton MacKinnon, author of <u>Nomading: Why Some Of Us Leave</u>, former job developer

"A very practical, hands-on guide to help you land a job that matches your interests and strengths. A must-read for recent college grads and those finding themselves back in the marketplace after being with one employer for a long time."

     — Clyde Stutts, Ph.D, Executive Vice President, DHR International Executive Recruiters

"Very detailed with helpful information that can be quickly accessed and practiced, and thoughtful enough to really allow the student to put together a game plan, and that's what it's really about — putting together a game plan for the future, identifying their target, really researching the company, accessing their own strengths and weaknesses, practicing in preparation, and executing the game plan on game day."

     — Joe Standridge, Lecturer, Sonoma State University, School of Business and Economics, CPA

"Ken provides useful direction for students graduating from academia into the real world. He goes beyond theory and provides a practical approach for young/entry level professionals to take as they begin their careers. Ken's unique experience as both a recruiter and college educator provides specific direction to demystify that scary next step in young people's lives. Congratulations and thank you, Ken, for undertaking a tall task and creating something useful for so many."

     — Joseph Laudari, Independent Executive Search Consultant

"Ken Heinzel provides an excellent look at many of the most important aspects of the job search, from the very basics to using sophisticated skills to

advance one's career. I wish I had this book years back, as it would have been a great resource when I was a job developer, placement manager, workforce planning and recruitment manager, and of course as a job seeker. Considering the current job search situation today, this will be a bible for many."

"Excellent, well-structured guide for students and recent grads. This book should be required for all graduating seniors."

Private Notes
of a
Headhunter

Proven Job Search and Interviewing Techniques for College Students & Recent Grads

Kenneth A. Heinzel

ISBN: 0988493608
ISBN-13: 9780988493605

Pythian House Publishing, Santa Rosa, California

DEDICATION

To the American College Student.
It is you who makes this country great

To my wife, Inese, whose creativity, editorial skills, dedication
and discipline made this book possible.
You are the light of my life.

ACKNOWLEDGMENTS

A book is very rarely a creation of one person.

Almost all are a collaboration of one kind or another, even if the collaboration is an impersonal or a distant one over time.

This book's foundation is built upon the bedrock of personal collaborations that have occurred throughout the half-century of my adult life. Most of the partners in this library of names shall remain nameless because there is not space enough here to specify the hundreds who have directly or indirectly affected who I am today as I wrote this book.

That said, here in a broad sense is a profound Thank You to the individuals and groups who shaped who I am as the author of this book: My beloved parents; my high school teachers, the Irish Christian Brothers at Brother Rice High School in Chicago; The Western Golf Association, and the Evans Scholars Foundation; my fraternity brothers at the University of Illinois; my many excellent instructors at the University of Illinois and Northern Illinois, where I first began to teach in the classroom; officer mentors and friends in the United States Army, members of my personal support group who helped me through challenging career changes; many close friends among the Xerox Alumni; job candidates, clients and fellow recruiters who put their trust in me as a headhunter; students at Sonoma State University who enabled me to be a student again as well as an teacher; friends and family for their support.

Special specific thanks go out to my professor colleagues at SSU who gave me guidance and encouragement: Professors Robert Girling, Joe Standridge, Doug Jordan, and Liz Thach.

In the world of executive recruiting, Joe Laudari and Clyde Stutts. In the writers' world, author Brent MacKinnon. In the management world, Frank Tastevin from UCSF.

And to my lovely and irreplaceable editor and wife, Inese

CONTENTS

What If ... you're naturally shy?

What If ... things start to go bad in the interview?

What If ... you get a bad interviewer?

What If ... you've been fired or laid off?

Final Thoughts

Multi-tasking and Cognitive Learning – Pros & Cons

Feed Your Creativity

Social Media and Networking

Social Media Sites – Potential Red Flags

Facebook, LinkedIn, Monster and the Job Search

Information vs, Knowledge

Useful Job Search Internet Sites

FOREWORD

For the last four decades I have been privileged to be the teacher and mentor to hundreds of students eager to learn what it takes to find a job and build a successful career. During this time the employment market has been a roller-coaster mirroring the shifting sands of the economy and leaving students uncertain about their job prospects. Each year students' anxieties about finding a job mounted. Students want to work with good companies but are just not sure how to go about the job search. Fortunately, about five years ago, my colleague Ken Heinzel began developing a seminar based on his extensive experience as an executive recruiter. I invited Ken to present his seminar to my class of graduating seniors. The result was an instant hit with the students. Invariably students remark that Ken Heinzel's session is the single most valuable class meeting of the semester. (I know what you are thinking—what am I doing during the other class meetings!)

Now Ken has made his excellent material available to all in his new book Private Notes of a Headhunter: Proven Job Search and Interviewing Techniques for College Students and Recent Grads. What he offers, and what I have not found in any other book, is a demystification and deconstruction of the job interview seen from the vantage point of an executive recruiter who was also a college professor. It provides a wealth of information on just what to do to get and succeed in the interview as well as the biggest mistakes students tend to make in interviewing and how to avoid them. Private Notes of a Headhunter is a book that provides a guide through the rites of passage from the university to the professional world.

The reader benefits from Ken's years of combined experience and he readily brings together information from both the academic and professional worlds explaining to the student in easy to understand language just what they need to do to get their ideal job. What really brings the book alive are Ken's real-life examples, most drawn from his own extensive experience. The book covers the gamut of the job interviewing process while providing "insider" information concerning the interview process. Moreover, for the first-time job seeker it deals with the pitfalls, fears, and self-doubts, while sharing advice on just what they must do in order to overcome any obstacles.

The book is an easy read; in fact, it can be read and digested in a couple of hours. Read it and then start preparing to find a good job with a good company!

– Robert H. Girling, Ph.D.

Robert H. Girling, Ph.D. is professor in the School of Business and Economics at Sonoma State University where he has taught for over 35 years. His latest book is <u>The Good Company</u> *(Hill Press, 2012).*

INTRODUCTION

Pablo Picasso, asked by a young artist how long it took him to complete a particular painting, replied, "About three hours and thirty years" — the culmination of a lifetime of dedicated work and talent.

As for <u>Private Notes of a Headhunter</u> ... I figure nineteen months and nineteen years, and counting.

Success is a result of education, commitment, skill and practice. My combined experience as a successful executive recruiter (headhunter) and university instructor serve as the bona fides for this book. Working both sides of the proverbial fence – academia and the business world – has given me a unique perspective and understanding of the all-important transition from college student to career seeker. Here you will get insider information and instruction, tailored expressly to your needs as recent and soon-to-be college grads entering the most challenging job environment in many years.

Seeing how unprepared many of my students were for the work world "out there," I began, years ago, to deliver student-centered lectures on how to do job searches and succeed in the job interview. Soon students in other classes and student organizations were asking me to coach them in the interviewing process. Colleagues asked me to present my ideas and methods in their classes. Eventually, what began as a series of talks and lectures evolved into a seminar — and now this book — on the job search and interviewing techniques based on my professional experience as an independent executive recruiter, targeted specifically to the college audience.

Chances are that in that roster of courses you've taken, not one was focused on how to look for a job effectively or how to interview successfully, much less how to land the job of your dreams. That's why you picked up this book, isn't it? — to find out how to make that transition, how to turn that GPA and all those college courses into career gold.

Think of this book as that one all-important course — focused entirely on transforming you, a successful student, into a successful career employee — from a thorough analysis of critical factors in effective interviewing to exclusive pointers about job interviewing that, as a hiring manager and headhunter, I have implemented and honed over the years. The information and the skill-building examples and exercises have been successfully road-tested by students and job-seekers just like you. These techniques work because they are based on real people, real experiences.

I will also provide you with a clarification and expansion of certain factors about interviewing that have not been developed well in mainstream media. Some of the information there is misguided, naïve, or in some cases just plain wrong.

The lessons you will learn here have worked for others, and they will work for you. With your degree, you have demonstrated your potential to do a great job in your chosen field. What you may lack is experience, especially experience in interviewing for that great job. I'm going to make up for that lack by sharing my experience with you. Throughout the course of this book, I will be your personal recruiter.

STRATEGIES, SKILLS AND STREET SMARTS

The interview process is a process of elimination, getting down to the final two or three candidates, and then picking who is perceived to be the best. Every positive aspect about you not only increases your chances for success but also may actually eliminate some negatives about you or your background. This book will help you avoid several common pratfalls and make you aware of some positive things you can do to increase your chances of success.

Reading and applying the techniques in this book, you will:

- Understand the job interview process from both sides — yours and the interviewer's.

- Learn to get over the idea that the job search process should be "fair." It's not.

- Learn to tap into all available resources and support to make the job search and interview process more enjoyable and effective.

- Learn what interviewers want, and how to convince them you have it.

- Develop a personal action plan for successful job interviews.

- Practice and implement proven interviewing techniques.

- Increase your chances of getting the job vs. your competition.

QUICK TIPS AND SHORT CUTS

Sorry, but there are no effective "quick tips" or "short cuts" to mastering the job interview. The ones I've seen are superficial, misleading, and even dangerous, in the respect that they can hypnotize you into thinking that the job interview will be easy and you can be successful with just a few short bits of advice. It just doesn't work that way.

The interview is the equivalent to the toughest final you took in your senior year. There were no gimmicky short cuts there. You know the amount of preparation, applied study, hard work, and critical thinking it took you to get a super grade in the keystone course of your major.

There is no short cut to "ace'ing" the interview, either. The only short cut, if you don't prepare properly, is to the unemployment line.

If you insist on quick tips and short cuts to the job search and interview, don't buy this book. Go elsewhere for advice. The successful job interview is one of the most important events in your professional career. Treat it as such.

MY QUALIFICATIONS

When choosing a book about the job search, and especially the interviewing process, look for authors that have appropriate qualifications. Here are mine:

- A decade of executive recruiting experience as a headhunter
- Twenty years in industry as sales rep and sales manager in large corporations and small businesses
- Small business entrepreneur
- Ten years as a university lecturer in business and marketing
- Leadership experience as an officer in the United States Army

Many, if not most, books on the market about the job search and specifically the interview process are written by people whose profession is to write "how-to" books. They may have no practical experience in the subject matter, nor have been professional recruiters / headhunters, or managers ... especially hiring managers.

I understand the interviewing process on both sides of the table, having placed people across the full spectrum of hiring, from homeless people in entry-level jobs (as a placement volunteer), to high-tech executives making six figures. I have taught/counseled/coached and guided college students with their studies and career aspirations and have an affinity for students and recent grads, and always will.

What I'm proud of most is that I have helped a lot of people get very good jobs and made a great deal of money in the process.

I can help you, too.

PREVIEW

The source material that makes the information in this book worthwhile and truly relevant to you is built on prevalent needs of today's student job-seekers and of potential employers, compiled from interviews I conducted with students as well as representatives from a variety of hiring companies.

The **Student Question Forum** presents the top interests and concerns of college students and recent grads. The **Job Fair Survey** provides current inside information directly from the people that hire people like you. These actual questions and comments from students as well as company recruiters *in their own words* will, I hope, make the lessons even more meaningful.

Following are **highlights** from the **Student Question Forum** and the **Job Fair Survey.** You'll find both studies in their entirety in **Appendix E**, at the end of the book.

STUDENT QUESTION FORUM

During some of my recent seminars at Sonoma State University, I asked students at the conclusion if they would like to participate in a question-naire (below) about the seminar and about the job search and interviewing. Participation in the questionnaire was entirely voluntary and anonymous

---

JOB SEMINAR QUESTIONNAIRE/2012

(Prepared by Kenneth A. Heinzel, MS)

1. What <u>concerns you most</u> about interviewing for a job?

2. What <u>resources have you used</u> so far in researching how to interview for a job?

3. If you had <u>one question to ask an expert</u> about an upcoming job interview, what would it be?

4. What would be <u>most useful</u> for you, as a college student, in <u>a job interview book</u>?

5a. What has been <u>most useful</u> to you in this job interview seminar?

5b. What would you want to <u>learn more about</u>?

6. Any other questions, comments, or thoughts?

This questionnaire is for research purposes, data collection and illustration in the development of the job interview seminar and written materials. May I have your consent to use your responses? Only your first name and initial would be used.

Signed: _____ Date _____

The students' responses revealed a broad array of observations and deeply felt concerns. By far, the four greatest concerns of student job interviewees were:

1. **Stress and stress management.** Closely related concerns were: fear of failure in the interview; nervousness; not answering questions properly; committing a gaffe (i.e., "looking like a dummy").

2. **Questions**... specifically, those asked by the interviewer, and how to prepare answers for them. Also, what questions should students/candidates ask of the interviewer.

3. **Beating the competition**. How do I stand out?

4. **First impressions.** What are they expecting?

I've provided a short answer for each of the four top Forum questions, followed by a chapter reference where you will find a more complete answer. Again, following are selected questions/answers. The complete study is found in **Appendix E**

Stress and Stress Management

Q: *Can you give me some stress management tips?* (Adam G.)

Short Answer: Ask an experienced person in your support group what they do to relieve stress before the interview. Review stress-relieving techniques such as deep breathing and visualization. See also: "Your Support Group" (Ch. 2) and, "What if you're waiting for the interview and you get nervous" (Ch. 8).

Q: *How do you respond to a question that you are truly stumped on?* (Christine A.)

Short Answer: Ensure you understand the question to begin with; if not, calmly ask the interviewer to repeat or rephrase question so you understand it — this will also give you more time to think. Then give the best answer you can. See also: "The Importance of Rehearsing" (Ch. 3).

Questions Asked by the Interviewer

Q: *What do I do if I'm surprised by a question?* (Heather S.)

Short Answer: Expect to be surprised by a question at some point in the interview. The interviewer wants to see how you handle being surprised. Learning to think on your feet is the important lesson here. It's important to relax, take a few moments to think of the answer before you respond. Mock interviews can help a lot to develop poise. See also: "Mock Interviews" and "The Importance of Rehearsing" (Ch. 3).

Questions Asked by the Interviewee

Q: *What questions should I ask at the end of the interview?* (Kersti O.)

Short Answer: "If you were to hire me, what's the most important thing I could do for you in the first 90 days on the job?" See also: "Questions to Ask the Interviewer" (Ch. 5).

Beating the Competition and Standing Out

Q: *How can I make myself stand out if I don't have an outstanding background?* (Maura B.)

Short Answer: There are several things you can do. One is to have questions prepared to ask the interviewer that relate to the specific job in question. See also: "Questions to Ask the Interviewer" (Ch. 5).

First Impressions

Q: *Do interviewers really make up their minds in the first 10 minutes of the interview?* (Joelle E.)

Short Answer: Interviewers form an impression of what they think about you early in the interview, but usually won't make a final decision at that point unless you did or said something awful. They will make a final decision about you as a serious candidate sometime within the next hour after they have gathered more information. Still, immediate impressions are very important. See also: "The Importance of First Impressions" (Ch. 3).

OTHER IMPORTANT QUESTIONS

How do you know if you are prepared for the interview?

Q: *Is there a way of knowing which questions to prepare for?* (Jesus V.)

<u>Short Answer:</u> You will never know in advance the specific questions that an interviewer will ask. However, the Basic Four Questions (Ch. 5) are always asked in some form during every interview. Having answers prepared for these will give you a big edge. See also: "Other Questions You Might Be Asked" (Ch. 5).

Q: *How will I know when I'm really prepared for the interview?* (Ethan C.)

<u>Short Answer:</u> Have you researched the company enough that you could write a short paper about them? Do you have at least six or seven questions prepared to ask them? See also: "The Basic Reason Why Companies Want to Hire You" (Ch. 3).

The Interview Going Bad and Body Language

Q: *What are the signs of the interview going south, and what can I do about it?* (Teal J.)

<u>Short Answer:</u> There are several. Among them, miscommunication of any kind, and negative body language exhibited by the interviewer. See also: "What if things start to go bad in the interview" (Ch. 8).

Q: *What are the keys to turning around a negative interview?* (Kyle S.)

<u>Short Answer:</u> When things have obviously gone bad, take charge and ask the interviewer if you can re-visit a question they just asked to clarify what you said. Also, have something dramatic to show them. See also: "Your 30-Day Plan" (Ch. 4).

Networking

Q: *Can you give me an example of how to get an interview, when I couldn't otherwise get one?* (Meagan D.)

Short Answer: Your best resource for getting an interview is your own personal network, which has your personal support group at its core. At least 70% of job leads come from this source. See also: "Networking and Your Support Group" (Ch. 2).

Lack of Experience

Q: *How do I present myself so that my age or lack of experience won't hinder me?* (Meagan D.)

Short Answer: Even if you have had no direct job experience yet, you still have accomplished things in the past that produced results of some kind. These results are your best strengths, which must be expressed in terms of benefits to the interviewer and their company. See also: "How to Become an Effective Salesperson... of You" (Ch. 4).

Q: *How should I describe my experience and myself in a professional way even if I do not have a lot of experience?* (Joelle E.)

Short Answer: Be well rehearsed and knowledgeable about your personal strengths. Tell the interviewer how these strengths will solve their problems as far as this job is concerned. See also: "The Basic Reason Why Companies Want to Hire You" (Ch. 3).

JOB FAIR SURVEY

In March 2012 I went to a Campus Job Fair at Sonoma State that brought together approximately 50 companies as well as representatives of the Armed Services.

My objective was to get *first-hand information* from interviewers and company recruiters about what they look for in today's college student/recent grad job candidates. While the sample of companies in the survey was small, the respondents provided valuable insight from an interviewer's point of view. And, significantly, what interviewers and recruiters said they want in candidates was the same, across the board.

Companies/entities participating in my survey:

Calix	**Nelson Personnel**
Fireman's Fund Insurance	**Northwestern Mutual**
G.C. Micro	**Target**
Hertz	**United States Army**
Kohl's	**Vector Marketing**

Questions and Responses

Question 1: What are some of the important things that you look for in today's student job candidates?

Responses:

- **Are they prepared for the interview?** (Every company mentioned this.) Do they have knowledge about our company? Have they done their research? Do they have prepared questions?
- Do they communicate well?
- Are they enthusiastic about interviewing with us?

Question 2: If you had one piece of advice to give to a candidate, what would that be?

Responses:

- **Come prepared!**
- Network with recent grads.
- Have a good attitude and show confidence.

Question 3: What are some of the things that turn you off to a student candidate?

Responses:

- **Not being prepared**.

- Not having questions, especially at the end of the interview.

- Lack of confidence.

Question 4: Do you have any other observations or impressions of today's student candidates?

Responses:

- Respondents said that they expect most candidates to be nervous at the beginning of the interview. Most mentioned that they would do their best to put the candidate at ease by: starting with casual conversation (small talk); giving them a preview of what's to come in the interview; stating that they realize that the candidate is new to the interview process and try to calm them down. One interviewer's policy is to send an e-mail in advance to give the candidate a general idea of what to expect in the interview.

STUDENTS' FEEDBACK ABOUT THE JOB INTERVIEWING SEMINARS

- *Thank you so much! I feel like we got a real inside look.* (A. B.)

- *Thank you for taking the time to provide helpful information from [your] experience.* (Ricardo R.-A.)

- *Thank you for giving an inside view of how a headhunter thinks.* (Anonymous)

- *Great presentation, Ken! We hope to have you back again. I wish they taught this in school.* (Adam G., President, University Finance Club, Sonoma State University)

- *Thought it was very informative. Great lead to my first career interview.* (Dave T.)

- *This seminar was a great help, and I plan on using these techniques in my upcoming job search.* (Ryan S.)

- *Thanks for showing how to finish and follow up with an interview.* (Justine S.)

- *Now I know the best way to prepare for an interview.* (Ria L.)

- *Following Ken's interview secrets will help you get a job. I have used them to great success.* (Nate L.)

To review the **Student Question Forum** and **Job Fair Survey** in their entirety and read more of what other students/job-seekers and potential employers had to say, go to **Appendix E.**

CHAPTER I
GENERAL REFLECTIONS ON THE JOB SEARCH

"Each venture is a new beginning." (T.S. Eliot)

IT'S A WHOLE NEW BALL GAME OUT THERE

The job search and the interview process have been key components to a healthy economic life in America. But how the game is played has changed a great deal. Gone, for the most part, are the days of long-term employment with one company. Job-hopping is becoming the norm these days, with a worker averaging between 8 to 12 jobs in a lifetime.

Also gone, to a great extent, is company loyalty to employees. This trend started in earnest in the serious recession of 1981-82 and became pervasive during the decade of the nineties and into the first decade of the new millennium. In many company annual reports prior to 1982 or so you will see a statement like "Our employees at XYZ Corporation are our most valuable asset." You won't find many statements like that today, or if you do, it's usually token PR claptrap that sounds good but has no basis in fact. (After all, annual reports aren't supposed to make you laugh out loud.) For the truth, check out what these same corporations did to their employees during the last recession or their last RIF (reduction in force). Did they fight to retain employees, or did they lay them off in large numbers?

So the employee, after two and a half decades of continual, serious layoffs, mergers, acquisitions, closings, the dot.com disaster, the recent recession, etc., has little loyalty either.

Are you looking for your first job? Your first raise? Or your first promotion? Even if you currently have a good job you can still benefit from selected chapters of this book. Many of the topics will help you get your first (or next) raise, and your next promotion. Essentially, you are in the process of "interviewing" from your first day on the job for both of these. Like it or not you have to get good at the job search, and its most critical component, the interview, if you are to do well professionally, economically, and personally... that is, to be happy in what you do.

In 2008 we had what was almost a cataclysmic financial disaster, the unofficial start of the "great recession," so named since it was the most extensive recession in America since the Great Depression. Technically, it began in December 2007 and ended in June 2009. That's 18 months, far longer and greater than the recessions of '81-'82, '90-'91 and 2001, with the average recession since World War II lasting about 11 months.

Although the great recession officially ended in June 2009, the lingering effects will go on for years as far as unemployment is concerned, possibly into 2015. The effects of recessions caused by the reckless decisions of financial institutions tend to go deeper and last longer than those of run-of-the-mill business-related recessions and those caused by governmental, monetary and fiscal practices.

"We have a monster jobs problem, and young people are the biggest losers," writes Andrew Sum, an economist and director of the Center of Labor Market Studies at Northeastern University. "Their really high levels of underemployment and unemployment will haunt young people for at least another decade."[1]

Richard Freeman, an economist at Harvard University, concurs. "Young people will be scarred and they will be called the 'lost generation' – in that their careers would not be the same way [sic] if we had avoided this economic disaster." [2]

Bluntly put, if you do not have a well-developed action plan in place at the start of your search, you are not likely to succeed in getting a good job in this market. This plan is as important as any paper or senior project you will

---

1   Yen, Hope. "A Generation Lost? Check the Basement." <u>Press Democrat</u> 15 Sept. 2011.
2   Ibid.

ever produce in college, and more. Outlining, researching, developing and following through on your action plan can guarantee you that "A" in nailing the job interview. In Chapters 2 and 3 you'll learn all about how to create your personal action plan, a stratagem that will dramatically increase your chances of getting the job you want.

You have to be better than your competition. The race to the great jobs is not always won by the smartest people. It's won mostly by people who won't make the mistakes that their competition makes, who know things about the job search and especially the interview process that others don't, and who know what to do with "insider" information that helps them win in the interview process. I will help you understand and implement all three of these vital advantages you must have over your competition, and help make you the one that wins.

YOU MUST BECOME THE CEO OF YOUR LIFE

The discussion of the interview process is part of a larger process that you must undertake. If you are to be successful in life, especially in the world of work, you must become your own CEO.

In effect, everyone is their own CEO, but there are plenty who don't do a very good job of it. If you challenge this statement, just click on your favorite media page for daily examples of personal corporate failures.

Why is becoming your own CEO of your personal career path essential to your success? New York Times columnist Thomas Friedman took a frank look at this important topic in his July 12, 2011 column, "The Start-up of You." Friedman wrote that today's employers are looking for "... people who not only have critical thinking skills to do the value-adding jobs that technology can't, but also people who can invent, adapt and reinvent their jobs every day in a market that changes faster than ever."[3] This is what CEOs do.

You're the only one that's responsible for you. In a job interview, you have to take responsibility for your future success and pitch your **personal value proposition** (covered in Chapter 4) to a hiring manager, interviewer, or venture capitalist officer, *and* explain it in terms of benefits that will show

---

3   Friedman, Thomas. "The Start-up of You." New York Times 12 July 2011.

them how you can **help them make, raise, or save money**. If you don't take the strengths that make up your personal value proposition and translate them into benefits that relate specifically to the hiring company, then you will have pitched a value proposition that won't be distinguishable from that of many other college grads. You're your own CEO now, so think smarter than the other guys.

In the final analysis, a job search is also a search for yourself. It requires not only a sure knowledge of the territory, but also knowledge of who you are and what you really want in life, if you are to make the right decisions. You must muster your courage, stamina, training, education, insights — indeed, all of your life experience and self-knowledge — to successfully undertake and complete one of life's most demanding and lonely endeavors, the job search and the interview.

THINK OF LIFE AS ONE BIG INTERVIEW

Get used to interviewing, because you will be doing it continually for the rest of your working life.

Recessions are a normal part of the American capitalist system, and you will probably experience at least five or six in your working lifetime, and the layoffs and overall job reduction they bring on. In addition, like most Americans, you, too, will probably change jobs 8 – 12 times in your forty-plus years of working, and probably change careers at least once, maybe twice. (By career change, I don't mean moving within one field, such as from one engineering job to another, or one nursing job to another. A true career change means moving from one work discipline to a completely different one, such as changing from law to education, or changing from a bank officer position to running a retail grocery store.)

The average job tenure in the US is now 4.4 years, according to the Bureau of Labor Statistics.[4] In specific sectors such as technology, it's less than four years and in the broad category of sales, it's less than three. In a very practical sense you will always be in job search mode actively or passively for the rest of your working life.

4   US Bureau of Labor Statistics. 20 Aug. 2011 <http://www.bls.gov>

My personal stats mirror the national trends. Not counting my military service after graduate school, I've had nine jobs and changed careers three times during 41 active working years. My longest job tenure was twelve years with a major corporation, and the shortest was with a small software company in San Francisco for a year and a half. This works out to a mean tenure of 4.6 years. Your experience will probably be close to that.

THE JOB SEARCH PROCESS

There are several elements that make up the job search process, starting with an honest self-evaluation to reaching out for support from others. Read through the following list of process fundamentals. How much have you already accomplished? What do you need to do? Write down your answers to the *Job Search Fundamentals* in a journal or notebook as completely as you can at this point, and then revisit them from time to time, to gauge how you're doing:

Job Search Process Fundamentals

Know yourself as best you can, from your strengths and weaknesses to your overall outlook on life and what you want. Consider:

- Who *are* you?

- What are your skills and talents? (Consider taking a few aptitude tests to help you discover what you might be good at.)

- How important is money to you?

- How important is free time to you? (work/life balance)

- How important is happiness to you?

- How comfortable are you with taking risks?

- How are you in stressful situations? How do you deal with shyness?

- How would you rate yourself in the four personal attributes of the job search: Desire, Preparation, Persistence, and Attitude?

- How do you respond to change, such as the change of environments (e.g., from university to company or corporate)?

Next:

- Have you chosen a career field (at least for the present)?

- Have you targeted specific companies for getting interviews?

- Have you created a resume? (See Ch. 2)

- Have you developed your personal network and support group? (Ch. 2)

Who Are You?

If you don't have a reasonably good idea of who you are, what's important to you, and what makes you happy, this is the first place to spend some time and energy. Why? If you don't have at least a basic idea about these three things, you probably won't interview well.

Asking yourself, "Who am I?" is a huge undertaking and perhaps even a little intimidating. So look at yourself as a job candidate. From this perspective you'll want to reflect on your likes and dislikes, aptitudes and life experiences, including how you respond to change. We change constantly and sometimes a lot in a relatively short period of time. Looking back to your freshman year, for instance: would you say that you have changed much since then?

We are also driven by outside events in our lives, for example, transitioning from high school to college; graduating from college and transitioning to the work world; moving; relationships. National and even world events may touch you personally, too, such as the state of the economy when you launch your career search; which companies are hiring; how much money you can expect to earn, and so on.

Aptitude Tests

Taking aptitude tests can be helpful. Some of the tests mentioned in the well-known work <u>What Color is Your Parachute?</u>[5], or any number of available tests at your university career center or on the Internet can be a starting point. But remember, aptitude tests are just one tool in determining who you are and what you may be good at.

---

5   Bolles, Richard. <u>What Color is Your Parachute? 2012.</u> Ten Speed Press, 2011.

Money – The Personal Implications

You can't escape the importance of money in your personal life. In my experience and the experience of my headhunter colleagues, the main reason people change jobs — by far — is money. It's not necessarily because they hate their boss, or that they are bored, or that they can't get a promotion, or that their commute is killing them, or that they are working far too many hours. Do some people change jobs for any of these reasons? Yes, some do. But for the most part, it's about the money. Very few people are motivated by one or more of the above items enough to accept the same or less money in another job. They just don't do it unless they are looking for a life-changing event, such as changing careers.

Nevertheless, studies have shown that money or the quest for more money brings only temporary satisfaction. Once the new goal or prize is secured, satisfaction and happiness start to wane, and a renewed quest for more money is soon begun. In short, when it comes to humans and money, more is never enough. For those who are really obsessed about money, how much they earn is just a way of keeping score in a game of competition with their peers.

I say that you have to be aware of the importance of money in both your professional and private lives but you don't have to be a slave to it. A way to check the influence of money on you as a person is to follow the advice in Marsha Sinetar's influential book, Do What You Love and The Money Will Follow.[6]

The Importance of Happiness

Happiness is what we all are pursuing in the long run, isn't it? The Declaration of Independence states this explicitly. When we seek money, or a good relationship, or a great job, what we are really seeking is happiness.

Happiness, like chemistry between people, is unique to the person(s) involved. We each have to define it for ourselves and be prepared to redefine it throughout our lives as our needs, wants and situations change. What are the things that are worthwhile and bring happiness (call it personal

---

6   Sinetar, Marsha. Do What You Love and the Money Will Follow. Dell Publishing, 1987.

satisfaction) to you in your work, and why is this so important? For one thing, you will be facing over 2,000 or more Monday mornings in your working years. Waking up to a bad feeling about your job is no way to live a life, and it sure isn't happiness.

Consider your work/life balance carefully. Some jobs or professions require 70-hour work weeks; if you like what you do, that is fine, but you are also giving up YOUR TIME and ability to do things outside of work, such as being with family, hobbies, friends, etc. It's a tradeoff ... so make that tradeoff consciously.

Happiness, well-being, and a sense of satisfaction about what you do *in your work* tend to be tied to the following:

- Doing something productive that provides personal fulfillment
- Doing something that is challenging and supports personal growth
- Recognition other than money
- Reasonably good compensation
- Accountability and the authority that should come with it
- A good chance for professional growth along a clearly identified career path
- Freedom to take action or make judgments
- A chance to make a difference in the lives of others
- Working with people that respect and like you

This is not intended to be an all-inclusive list, but without most of these factors you will find yourself moving on in fairly short order to another job and possibly a career change.

THE KEY ELEMENT OF THE JOB SEARCH: ATTITUDE

The attributes essential to a *successful* job search are **Desire**, **Preparation**, and **Persistence**. But it is your **Attitude** throughout the process that clinches it.

Case in Point:

A friend and colleague of mine in my early days as a salesman at Xerox spoke at the graduation of my basic sales class at the company. Jim J. was already a highly successful sales manager with a dynamic presence and energy that electrified everyone he came in contact with. He was glad to share his wealth of knowledge and experience to help us begin our careers. Jim's central message was clear: "Controlling your attitude toward your job here and in your life in general will be essential for your success. It's the only thing that you truly control yourself."

Jim J. knew what he was talking about. He practiced what he preached and a decade later became the president of World Savings, a company that, at the time, was one of the largest financial institutions in America.

I'm continually reminded of how complex a thing attitude is. Each of us ulti-mately must make the choices that determine how successful and satisfied we will be in life. No one else can do this for us.

However, since self-analysis is subjective, it's helpful to ask for an opinion from a trusted friend or colleague. Make that two or three people close to you, those who will give you some honest insight. They can spot things that you can't (or won't). Advice of a personal nature can be difficult to take, but an objective, straightforward evaluation of your attitude can be invaluable. A bad or indecisive attitude about how you deal with people or important issues can be spotted very quickly by an experienced interviewer and will eliminate you as a candidate. The opposite is also true. A genuine, positive attitude will directly affect your enthusiasm and energy, and this will come across imme-diately. A good attitude is the gateway to success in the interview.

The University Environment vs. the Work Environment

What you experience today in a university is an open, liberal, non-threaten-ing environment, deliberately created by faculty and university officials to encourage self-awareness, critical thinking and freedom of expression in a safe atmosphere. When you graduate and enter the job market, your envi-ronment will change radically and that change starts with the interview.

There are rules that you must obey, or you won't be admitted to the club of professional success. You won't like some of these rules, because they will be an uncomfortable change for you.

The most fundamental change from being a college student to an employee is, simply, it's no longer all about *you*. The primary mission of a university or college is your education and welfare, whereas the sole goal of a company or organization is to promote the company's interests and profits. As an employee, you contribute to that mission, but *you* are not the mission.

In addition, learning and adjusting to new standards of ethical behavior and company codes of conduct can be quite challenging. Adapting to the new rules of corporate culture, customs, ethics, relationships and expectations will be necessary for not only your success in the interview process, but also for your success (and perhaps even survival) in the job. Chapter 4 addresses company culture and Chapter 7 discusses the topic of ethics in detail.

Choosing a Career Field

As for as picking a field of endeavor or career field, it's crucial to determine as best you can right now what's important about the kind of work you want to do, and what will make you happy doing it ... "following your bliss," as scholar Joseph Campbell describes in the seminal book, The Power of Myth.[7] Studying something in theory and actually doing it in the work world are two very different things, and your major field of study in college may not lead you to a job that fulfills you. Can you have both? It depends on how well you know yourself ... and the field you are pursuing.

---

7   Campbell, Joseph, with Bill Moyers. Joseph Campbell and The Power of Myth. Anchor Books, 1991.

Case in Point:

Gerry G., a fraternity brother of mine at the University of Illinois, got a B.S. in architecture. Architecture is a very demanding course of study, but he had dreamed of being an architect for as long as he could remember so he didn't mind the effort he had to put into his studies. He had a high GPA when he graduated and had no trouble getting a job with a large architectural firm in downtown Chicago. However, after just a few years on the job, he became very unhappy. Despite all the determination, time, effort and expense that had gone into his degree, he found the working reality as an architect to be unsatisfying and draining. It wasn't the life he had imagined and he knew he had to make a change. He decided to "follow his bliss." What was it? He became a yacht salesman and moved to Florida. He spent his summers selling in Canada, wintered down south, and found his core happiness again.

I had a similar experience. I majored in advertising and loved every minute of it. When I started interviewing during my senior year, I quickly became aware that the real world of advertising was a cutthroat environment of intense pressure. Careers could be – and were – ruined in very short order unless you were successful in all of your projects all of the time. This was true even for recent college grads who were still learning the trade. Lose an account, lose your job. The driving force in the industry appeared to be making money, period. Agencies created a climate in which clients and employees moved around a lot which, it seemed to me, suggested little loyalty on the part of either. This was not a world I wanted to live in because I knew I wouldn't be happy in it.

As you continue to read this book you'll learn how I eventually found my "bliss" ... through self-exploration and career and life experience. So can you.

Targeting Specific Companies to Get An Interview

You obviously will be able to garner lots of information about public companies and even some private companies on the Internet. However, the information that's most valuable is much harder to find. That is, *what it's like working for a particular company day to day*, such as:

- Will you be given not just the responsibility but the authority and freedom to do your job?

- Is it a friendly, or at least a pleasant place to work?

- Can you have a future here (a career path) with a chance for promotion, or is the company turnover rate high?

- Will you be treated with respect, or is the place repressive?

- How is the company viewed in its industry: is it respected by its peers, or do other companies and individuals tend not to want to do business with them?

This is just a starter list to get you thinking.

Insider information about a company is hard to come by. Don't believe the opinions of current employees unless you know them personally and trust them. Some of them will probably only give you positive comments because they don't want to lose their jobs by denigrating the company. Others who are unhappy in their jobs will paint you an all-negative picture. Past employees are usually a much better source of information, as are vendors, suppliers, and customers of the firm.

On the other hand, Internet blogs are probably not trustworthy because the views expressed on these sites tend to be extreme, positive or negative. Companies have been known to plant positive comments from fictional people about themselves on blogs. Also, someone who was fired from a company might seek revenge by posting nasty remarks on the blog to try to get even.

TIP: Take the time to go to your network and see if you can get any of the "back door" information about the company. If you wind up being a serious candidate with any company, they will use their network to try to get the same kind of information about you.

INFORMATIONAL INTERVIEWS AND INTERNSHIPS

The **informational interview**, if you are lucky enough to get one, is an information-gathering meeting only. The basic goal of this pseudo interview is to get a real job interview, if not with this company, then one in the same industry.

An **internship** is the best informational interview you can get. It amounts to an open exchange between you and the company involved that hopefully leads to a final interview and a job offer. In an internship, since you are living the company experience, your interview questions will be answered in great detail. At some point during or near the end of the internship, you can make a very informed decision about whether or not you want to work at that company. If you decide that you do, you are absolutely loaded at that point with insider information. This will enable you to nail the interview for a permanent position.

Take action. NOW.

Don't wait to take action in your job search. Begin now. Researching career fields and companies, developing your resume, reaching out to your network and support group — each action is an important step forward toward your goal: the interview and the job offer. In your college courses you learned how to organize your work around the end goal of a polished term paper or project. The job search is that, and more.

Don't rely entirely on the plans you have already made for your future. The future has a nasty way of breaking the appointments we have made with it, and it can do so suddenly. You will have to continually change plans and appointments along the way from now on.

At the end of each week, during an active job search, you must list the actions that you took during that week. If your list is small, you are not doing a very good job for yourself, and you're kidding yourself about achieving success. Actively looking for a job is a full time job in itself.

Let's move on now to things that must be done prior to the interview.

CHAPTER 2
GETTING THE INTERVIEW

"The secret of getting ahead is getting started." (Anonymous)

In order to get an interview at your target companies, you need to do some prep work. Here's what we will discuss regarding your prep:

- Networking and your support group

- Recruiters and other professional helpers

- Resumes

- The HR department

- Getting to the hiring manager

NETWORKING AND YOUR SUPPORT GROUP

Who you know can be just as important to your career as what you know.

Case in Point:

A good example of this important point relates to the critical nature of networking to your career path. A former friend and associate of mine at Xerox, Barry P., provided me with an introduction to my first big account, a very fast rising software company in Silicon Valley during the late nineties. I heard through a friend that Barry had become a very successful manager there. Although I had not seen

Barry for several years, I called him as soon as I heard this, and explained that I was now an executive recruiter in the high-tech arena. He called me in, explained his company situation and what they needed in staffing, and I began presenting some candidates within a week or so. Knowing Barry is what got me into this account at a time when so many other recruiters could not get in. Over the next six years, Barry's company became my most profitable account by far.

Never underestimate the power of networking. Ever.

Searching for something as important as a job is a combination of chasing after it and sometimes waiting for it to find you. The problem is knowing when to do which.

If you look back at your recent history and find that you have not been doing a combination of both chasing and waiting, your search could wind up being longer than you had bargained for. Quiet moments alone for reflection and visualization of what you want to have happen are important to the waiting part. Creating your own personal network and support group and using them effectively are important elements of the chasing.

YOUR PERSONAL NETWORK

So, what is your **personal network**? Simply, it's any person or persons who can provide you with a lead that results in your getting a job. Anyone. If you're not sure how to start forming your network, start with your Facebook or other social media personal contacts and, if you are on the LinkedIn system, professional contacts.

Think of your network as a concentric set of rings at whose core is your personal support group. In this group are direct personal and/or business contacts, friends, and confidants. (See adjacent diagram.)

Everybody's network is very personal because it depends on your interpretation and experience of whom you define as *friend, associate, colleague, family, brother* or *sister* (not necessarily the biological kind), *acquaintance, partner, pal, confidant(e)*. The important thing for you is to draw up your own network design, preferably on paper, or in digital form.

Networking is not just contacts, it's also relationships. Contacts are a list of names to call, hopefully with a reference from someone you know. Relationships go much deeper than that. They involve a significant, positive history of sharing in the past, or perhaps an encounter in the past that was mutually rewarding, where some sort of trust was established. This might mean someone you helped in the past, or someone who may have helped you. The bottom line way to measure these relationships in a practical sense is to ask, *Would they be glad to take my call, or smile at an e-mail from me?*

Contacts are names in your greater network. Close relationships reside in your support group.

Your personal network and its center, your support group, is where you should spend the vast majority of your search efforts.

YOUR PERSONAL NETWORK

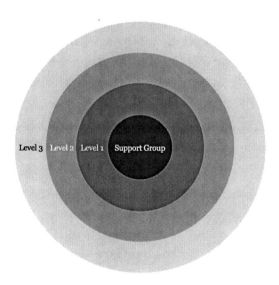

Support Group   A significant other; parents, siblings, extended family; close friends & neighbors; clergy & other authority figures who know you personally; business contacts whom you trust

Level 1   A member of a club, a religious or service organization you belong to (this is very fertile ground); professors who know you well; fraternity brothers or sorority sisters; someone you did a favor for in the past/someone who did a favor for you

Level 2   College classmates & alums; sports team members; casual social acquaintances and business associates; former co-workers; high school friends you see or call once a year; a friend of a friend whom you met at an event

Level 3   Virtual "friends," e.g., via Facebook, LinkedIn or other online communities; someone you met at a conference or job fair or similar event; a friend of a friend of a friend whom you met

YOUR SUPPORT GROUP

The most important element of your network, by far, is your **support group**. This group is aptly named: the essential elements that must be present here are **relationship** and **trust;** the willingness to work with you, even if it's just to make a key phone call; the capacity to understand your situation; the ability to take effective action; reasonable availability (access); the willingness and capability to give you comfort/support when and if you need it.

The only thing that your support group members may have in common (outside of family) is the personal stake they have in you, the relationship you have based on shared history, knowledge, trust and mutual esteem.

Individuals in your support group should be chosen by you, not the other way around. This is very important. Ask yourself, *Does this person open up to me?* Communication must be a two-way street. Trust is the key element necessary to be a member of this group because you will be opening yourself up to them and asking for (what else?) support. This will happen when you are in doubt about something you are about to do, or in pain because of something challenging that just happened to you. You will experience rejection during the interview process ... sometimes a lot of it. Even one rejection can be painful. Your support group is essential to easing the pain and preparing you to move on.

You probably have a support group already: close friends and relatives, associates you work with regularly, people that you get along with and can trust and confide in, not just someone that you have a beer with occasionally or think is cool. Mentors, too, like professors or current/past bosses with whom you have a rapport and keep in touch can also be in your core.

What your support group can do for you

Friends or associates who are also currently looking for work can be particularly supportive, act as sounding boards for ideas that you come up with, and be great sources of current information. Meeting with them once a week or so on a regular basis while you all are interviewing could provide all of the above benefits, and more. You can share "war stories," anecdotes about contacts and research, and/or what worked or didn't in a job search or an interview, and in that way you all gain from one another's experiences.

Occasionally support group members may just want to give you a contact name and a number to call, and that is valuable support. However, depending on your level of trust, you should also ask the member to call their contact, explain your situation to them and ask if it would be all right for you to call.

The Holy Grail for you, as far as the support group goes, is to get members, especially business peers, talking to one another about you. There's synergy and a multiplier effect when this happens. Interview set-ups are an almost certain outcome, if a job is available.

An interview obtained for you by an influential friend or a friend of a friend, not only gets you to the head of the interviewing line, but it also sets up a favorable bias in the interviewer toward you. This is the other side of the "it's not fair" coin, but it's one of the most important ways that people get jobs.

Why is this so? Since the interviewer responded to a friend /associate's request to give you an interview, they would have to come up with an important reason not to hire you if you have the basic qualifications for a job. And if they did and felt that you were not qualified for a particular job, they very likely would see if anything else was available in their company. It's a win-win situation, and a part of that synergistic effect.

When you're on the Internet, social sites like Facebook and professional networking sites like LinkedIn can be valuable sources of contacts. The danger here is that these sources are so easy to use that passive contact — emailing, texting — may cause you to spend a lot of time keyboarding when you should be *talking* to people directly, face to face or at least on the phone. Although both of these networks are excellent tools as far as they go, they have a seductive force about them that can make you believe that you are more effective in your search than you really are. You may find yourself spending hours trolling sites and getting sidetracked from your main aim, which must be to *connect* with people. Remember Ulysses and the siren's song.

One final, rather unusual side note: A pet can be a member of your support group. Seriously. Pets can sense fear, distress, anger, and can give you comfort and affection in time of need.

Case in Point:

A student of mine, who was a graduating senior at the time, told me in a counseling session that she was experiencing a very rough time in her life. Her parents were going through a nasty divorce after many years of marriage, and she was caught in the middle. In addition, she had recently lost a boyfriend who was killed in an automobile accident. Her course load was heavy (a little too heavy, to my mind) and this added to her stress level. She was a strong person outwardly, but she said she thought that she would "lose it." For some reason that she didn't understand at the time she impulsively adopted a puppy and she told me that they became very attached.

She said that getting that dog saved her life.

You will hear the word "No" many times during your working career, no matter how the word is paraphrased. Your support group – even a puppy – may be your lifeline.

Once you get a good job, don't forget your support group. It will take effort to keep in touch with them because "life happens" and in the rush of things these very important people could just slip away. Try to make contact at least once a year, as with the other important people in your network, just to say "hi." You'll never know when you'll need them again... and you *will* need them again.

SOURCES OF JOB LEADS AND YOUR PERSONAL NETWORK

Many, if not most, of the jobs that you land in your career will come from information and contacts discovered in your own personal network. Several studies bear this out.

Help-wanted ads or postings on the Internet, depending upon your source of information, account for 10-12% of the leads that result in someone getting a job. The US Department of Labor puts the figure at 5%. A small percentage of leads comes from trade shows, industry publications, and college career services. Head-hunters and employment agencies generate 6-8%. Most of the rest come from your own personal network. In my estimation, that means **close to 70% of all job placements come from personal networks and support groups.**

I want to reinforce this key point: *anyone,* no matter how obscure or how unlikely the circumstances, could lead to a contact that will lead to an interview. Let me cite two examples:

Case in Point:

The first is about how I got my job with Xerox Corporation (the "Google of the '70's"). After completing my military service at the Presidio in San Francisco I took a job back in my hometown, Chicago. After another brutal Midwest winter I swore to get back to the Bay Area. During the summer when I made the decision to leave my job and return to San Francisco, it happened that my aunt was throwing an informal backyard picnic for her neighbors. When my parents asked me if I would like to attend I rolled my eyes and was going to try to get out of going, but my aunt and uncle had always been very kind to me, so I figured, what the hell, I'll stop by for just a few minutes on my way to a Cubs game at Wrigley.

As it turns out, a guy at the party, whom I had never met or even heard about before, approached me while I was standing around having a beer with my uncle, and introduced himself as Charlie. He said that he was a sales manager for Xerox and that my aunt had told him that I was looking for a job. After a pleasant conversation that lasted a half hour or so, he invited me downtown the following week for a job interview.

I told him that I was planning on returning to the city of my dreams, and he said, OK, I'll call the San Francisco office tomorrow and see if I can set you up with an interview out there. I think he liked me.

Two weeks and three interviews later, I was offered a sales job in San Francisco, even though I had never sold anything in the business world before. That initial sales job and the three promotions that followed lasted almost 12 years. I'm sorry to say that I never saw Charlie again. But that chance meeting with him in my aunt's back yard changed my life.

The other story is about Nick, a nephew of a friend of mine who was living in a small resort town near Mt. Lassen in northern California. The town was used to experiencing the usual summer swell of tourists and shrinking back to a skeleton population during the winter. The great recession dried up even the usually lucrative seasonal jobs and left his small town in an employment desert.

After drifting between odd jobs for several months, Nick moved to the Bay Area in search of work. The job situation in Santa Rosa was also grim, at a 12% unemployment rate. After about two weeks, his cousin, whom Nick was rooming with, came home one night and told Nick that a coworker of his went to a local butcher shop to pick up something for dinner, and saw a help wanted sign in the window for an apprentice butcher. Nick went there the next day, got the job, and still works there today, as one of the store's managers. And he has earned his certification as a state meat inspector.

You will never know where good job leads will come from. Never. And some of them may come to you from the most unexpected, obscure sources and, some might say, in magical, even spiritual ways.

BOOKS ABOUT THE JOB SEARCH AND INTERVIEWING

Unlike a textbook which has been pre-selected for you, job search books, articles, blogs and the like are out there in the thousands for you to sort through and choose from. While the modus operandi of some will resonate more with you than others, gauge your choices on factors that will be key to the approach you will wind up taking in your job search as a result. Ask yourself: What sources are referenced? Are they creditable and reliable? How current is the information and how much is theory vs. real world? What are the author's credentials in the field? What can you learn here that you can apply immediately to your job quest?

While some of these resources provide excellent information, others are so elementary as to be useless at your stage of the game and still others are downright wrong in the advice they put out, which could seriously jeopardize your efforts if you follow it.

Let me give you a couple of examples of what to watch out for. I have seen advice in print that the candidate should "act" his/her way through the interview. This is exceptionally bad advice for several reasons. First, it prevents you from being yourself. Being yourself is where your true power resides, and acting out a role messes this up badly. Second, if the interviewer has any experience at all, or has even a mildly good talent at reading people, they will see right through you and you are probably toast. Third, since you have created an artificial situation, your judgment might be impaired and you could talk yourself into a job that you can't do well, and or will eventually hate. And who will show up on your first Monday morning, you or the actor?

Case in Point:

A good friend and associate of mine, Professor Joe S., recently told me that a student candidate decided to act his way through an interview that Joe had set up with one of his accounting firm contacts. After the interview, Joe contacted the client for an evaluation of the interview, and was told the following (I paraphrase): "I really liked your candidate. He was very personable, had good qualifications, but unfortunately, I felt that I never really met the guy." You guessed it – he didn't get a callback.

Unless you were nominated for an Oscar recently, leave the acting to professionals.

More bad advice is to memorize answers to frequently asked questions. Unless you have a very good memory, you will probably stumble when asked to respond to one of the 50-most frequently asked questions, the 100-most frequently asked questions, or the 500-most. Pick a number. There are extensive lists of these on the Internet. Don't memorize anything. Just review the *types* of basic questions asked so that you are generally familiar with them. Presumably, you didn't know what the questions were going to be on your final exams in school. How did you prepare? You studied the hell out of the appropriate course material.

Do the same with the target company's info. Know it cold, so you can come up with an answer to a general question on the spot. You don't have to memorize answers, and interviewers do not expect it; more than likely they want to see how you handle questions spontaneously. Study your research material. Practice. Repeat. Now go to your interview final and get your "A".

When we discuss the process of selling yourself in the interview in Chapter 4 (which uses a method that is very effective and relatively easy to use), you will be giving answers to the most important questions asked of you, and you don't have to memorize the answers to these. You already know them.

Much of the literature about interviewing, even the well-intentioned, well-constructed books, can be inadequate or unintentionally misleading. Authors who have interviewed a lot of people, but who haven't been interviewed much themselves in their careers, write some of this material. Educators, trainers and writers who have been on their own or in the same job for a long time come to mind.

In addition to being an interviewer and recruiter, I have been interviewed a lot over the years, through nine jobs, three career changes and twenty-plus years in industry. So what's the value of this? Let me ask you, did you ever take Driver Ed? Then you know what it's like to sit in the passenger seat, going along for the ride, like the Driver Ed instructor giving pointers to the student driver.

And you also know what it's like to finally *get behind the wheel and do the driving yourself.*

It's like the difference between being a lifeguard instructor and actually jumping in the water, risking your life to save someone. In my experience, the difference between being the interviewer as opposed to being the interviewee is like that.

There's a big contrast here: Seeing something from just one side of things, particularly the side where there is no threat, creates a pseudo reality of things that is mostly intellectual and devoid of the reality of "street smarts" that comes with risk taking and pressure to succeed.

RECRUITERS AND OTHER PROFESSIONAL HELPERS

Let's talk about professionals who can help you in both your job search and a successful interview. The main topic of discussion is **recruiters**. There are two main types: the first is the **company recruiter** and recruiting firms that deal strictly with recent college grads. They are the ones you will deal with for your first career job. The second type is the **executive recruiter**, or as they are known in the vernacular, **headhunters**. They are independent professionals whose job is to convince a "head" in one company to roll over into another. I was a successful headhunter for ten years, and I know the ins and outs of the trade.

After you have some experience under your belt in your first job, you should consider dealing with one of the responsible recruiters that you will find in the executive recruiting trade — this is where the true headhunter lives. But for your first career job right out of college, you will have to deal with company recruiters or recruitment firms that specialize in placing the just-graduated candidate. Headhunters won't be interested in you until after you have gained some experience because companies will not pay them to recruit you.

Most headhunters are ethical, reliable people who care a great deal about doing a great job for the client company and the job candidate. In my career I have met many of these highly professional people, several of whom acted as mentors to me while I learned the business. Not surprisingly, many of them are still in the business today, a decade after I left.

Because they are true professionals these recruiters take the time and make the effort to go beyond what the ordinary recruiter would do. *As a rule*, their procedure is to:

- Make sure that each candidate is properly vetted

- Meet each candidate personally or by phone (many excellent recruiters do much of their work by phone and electronic communication)

- Counsel each candidate about what to expect in the interview

- Be available to answer the candidate's questions at any time during and after the interview process

- Check up on the candidate if they are hired to make sure things are going well

- Maintain a professional relationship and regular contact with many candidates

- Assist in the negotiation process when a job offer has been extended to ensure a win-win solution for the company and candidate

- These practices serve to build long-term relationships with both the candidate and the client that lead to professional and financial success for all three parties.

That's the very positive side of the headhunter profession.

Now for the dark side, Obi Wan.

Make no mistake, the main objective of the executive recruiter/headhunter is to collect fees. For some of them, I'm sorry to say, that means that the candidate comes second, sometimes a very distant second. While many recruiters are decent, honest people operating in an extremely challenging — some would say cutthroat — career field (one that might be compared to the used car marketplace), this profession, as many others, attracts opportunists.

There is no regulation of any kind in the recruiting world, so the first rule of selecting an executive recruiter is to get a positive firsthand recommendation from a friend or associate whom you trust... that is, someone who has worked directly with the recruiter or was placed by them. To do otherwise is to trust your next career move to the unknown, like that used car purchase contract. You take it "as is." Next, ask them how long the headhunter has been in the business. Irresponsible fly-by-nighters usually don't last more than a year or so.

You may be thinking this criticism of executive recruiters is too harsh, yourself never having seen a shrunken head similar to yours hanging from someone's belt. From my years in the business, I've heard it all, from both sides. Let me give you a few specific examples, comments by some "successful" headhunters that reveal the true attitude of this unfortunate dark side of the force.

Case in Point:

One very powerful headhunter agency owner told me that the secret to success in recruiting was sheer volume. "Ken," he said, "Let me tell you, we're thieves selling s*** to idiots." Another headhunter's oft-repeated mantra: "Take the money. When in doubt, take the money." In other words, the welfare of the candidate and of the client was a distant second to their own. Unfortunately, statements like these are not unique in the business world.

After you have selected a recruiter, never, ever pay them for anything. Almost all legitimate recruiters are paid by the client (the hiring company) in the form of a fee that is based on a retainer (fee paid in advance), or on contingency (fee paid after successful placement). I have worked both as a retained and a contingency recruiter. A retained recruiter is safer for you since they have a true contractual obligation to the client and are probably more responsible and responsive than a contingency recruiter, but not always.

Some firms want to use as many recruiters as benefits them and will only support contingency recruiters, which means that they pay no fees to the recruiter until someone is hired and begins work. That someone isn't necessarily you, since the headhunter's chances for a fee increase with every candidate they put in front of the client. This atmosphere creates a scenario similar to that of the wild wild West, as far as you're concerned.

Unfortunately, some contingency recruiters will say anything to a candidate to get them to interview with a firm. They may not even have a contingency contract with the firm in question, so the object is to "throw as much crap up against the wall as possible, and hope some of it sticks." Thankfully, these types of recruiters don't last in the business very long, but they can do damage while there without suffering any kind of personal repercussions.

Other than placing you in a good job, the best thing that a recruiter can do for you is to introduce you to contacts. This means getting you interviews. These contacts should be hiring managers or people of influence that know the hiring manager. The third most valuable thing that a recruiter can do for you is to help you improve your interviewing skills.

A worthy recruiter will give you a complete briefing on the client company as it relates to your education and experience. They should tell you what you can expect from the interviewer, what personality type they are, and what types of questions they will ask. They will alert you to landmines and pitfalls that have eliminated other candidates. If you are inexperienced at interviewing but have great credentials, a good recruiter will want to meet with you face-to-face and put you through a mock interview. Realistically, they will only do this if they feel you are a very strong candidate for the position in question. Most of their work is done on the phone, especially with experienced candidates. Even for a responsible recruiter, it's still largely a numbers game.

Trustworthy, ethical recruiters are judged by three things: reputation, results, and integrity. Make sure you engage one of these after you do your due diligence, even if their fearsome title is headhunter.

Other Professional Helpers

Other than recruiters, other resources in the early years of the job search are **career marketers, employment agencies, college career centers**, and **public information** you can get on the Internet and in books and periodicals. It doesn't hurt to become a regular reader of major publications in your chosen field, either. These will clue you in to the culture, processes and jargon of the industry, as well as familiarize you with the top players and current news.

Career marketers and employment agencies, in most cases, will want to charge you something for their services. The charges can vary a lot, so what should you pay? The more they ask you to pay, versus their competition, the more you should be suspicious. During hard times, it's very common for desperate people who have been out of work for 6-plus months, and sometimes over a year, to have to pay three, four, five-thousand dollars or more for career advice, or employer contacts. Caveat emptor.

Never, ever pay more than five hundred dollars. Pay only for three things: 1) help in improving your interviewing skills, 2) your resume (especially if you're not used to writing resumes or your writing skills are shaky) and 3) contact names. Pay in installments only, so you can walk away at any time. If they say they have valuable contacts, fine. Pay for them in groups, one hundred dollars or so at a time, so you can judge how "valuable" they are. This won't take long to figure out.

If these contacts prove to be *not* valuable, walk. If there isn't an active, in-depth, ongoing interviewing development process from day one, take a hike. If they insist on a large up-front fee for their services, let's say more than $500, run.

As with recruiters, getting a reliable reference from your personal network or support group about any one of these agencies is essential. Disregard any preprinted references an agency gives you unless they are well known and beyond reproach, since they will be set up in advance to sound wonderful.

If you choose not to use an agency, or after you dump a bad one, go back to your support group — the people in the core of your personal network. Opportunities can change daily, and you just might surprise yourself by find-ing someone somewhere who knows of a good job that just opened up and can give you the name of the hiring manager, or better, make an introduc-tion call for you. This is the same advice that the "career marketer" will prob-ably give you after they have taken your money and wasted your time.

Your **college career center**, if it is a competent one, can provide you with some of the career help you need, even if it has been a few years since you graduated. They won't charge you for anything either, but you probably have to be a member of the university alumni association. The career center may be understaffed in bad budgetary times, but they should still be able to help you upgrade your resume, and hopefully provide you with local business contacts.

RESUMES

Although a detailed discussion of resumes is beyond the purview of this book (there is ample expert advice available from many sources, including book-stores, libraries, your college career center, and online), let me touch upon some key points.

A resume's role is to secure an interview. Period.

Content-wise, be sure that all of the key words in the job description for the position for which you are seeking an interview appear in your resume. This is essential to insure passing two possible filters: 1) that a potential employer giving your resume a quick look will spot the key words right away and 2) that the software scanning procedure that is used in mid-sized and large companies today for all candidate resumes, will register the key words and greenlight your resume.

A colleague of mine who is a VP at an executive recruiting firm, shares these key tips about resumes:

- Clarity and conciseness – Recruiters take about 20 seconds to screen a resume; too many words or a format that is not easily readable means rejection

- Focus on results, not just responsibility and quantify them, where possible, to demonstrate what you *did* vs. what you were responsible for

- Length – Work experience, education and special skills are important to include; a one to two-page resume is ideal

- Think of the resume as a fancy calling card. You should *always* carry at least two copies with you, even if you have to fold one up to put in the back pocket of your jeans on your way to your little brother's soccer match. His buddy Joey will be there and so will his father. Joey's dad might be looking for someone like you to fill a position that just opened up in his company. Stuff like this happens all the time.

A resume by itself never got anyone a job. That's right, never. Even if you're a former president of the United States, or you formulated the Theory of Relativity, prospective employers in both the profit and the non-profit world will want to meet with you personally to discuss your motives for wanting to work with them.

Let me say again, resumes are meant to lead to face-to-face meetings. These meetings are essential for discovering possible serious flaws in a particular personality or relationship. Even elite types sometimes don't work out in certain high placed positions. For everyday candidates, the failure rate is about 20% during the first year of employment. That's a fairly high percentage considering the time, expense and effort that companies put into the interviewing process. The failure rate would be even higher without a face-to-face.

A few comments here about the importance of spelling and punctuation. Don't trust your software's spell-check for errors in grammar, punctuation or spelling, and make sure you have three knowledgeable people check your resume for errors. In this respect your resume must be perfect, that's right, goddamned perfect. Grammatical mistakes and typos on the resume make you look sloppy, careless or uneducated, make a very bad first impression, and might cause your resume to be dumped instantly, since there are likely dozens of other candidates for this job. Even if you are invited in for an interview with a spelling or grammatical error or two on your resume, you step into the batter's box with strike one already on you. Bad odds.

A Word About Digital Resumes

The digital environment is the de facto way business is conducted today and it's common practice for companies to require applicants to submit their resumes and/or fill out their job applications online. Just click "send" and your resume is immediately delivered. No paper, no delay. No sweat. However, don't kid yourself into thinking that because it is *easy* that it is all you need to do. It isn't. The keyword screening software I mentioned earlier eliminates far more resumes than it passes on to a human reader. Your search may be over before you know it. Again, bad odds. If you understand that an electronically-distributed resume is just one small part of your job search process, then your odds have gone up, way up. (I will cover additional aspects of the job search and the Internet in Appendix C.)

Nicknames and Your Resume

It will be difficult to give up a personal descriptor such as a nickname in some cases when you're trekking through the job search jungle. It is endemic to American culture to attach nicknames to people. If the nickname projects a positive, even affectionate image (as most do), it can become a sign of acceptance from one's peer group. Of course, the opposite can occur if the nickname has a negative tone. Usually the person who is the object of a derogatory nickname will fade away from the peer group into exile.

So, to get a nickname can be a kind of badge of honor and shows that you have special status among friends and associates. You belong.

However, the nickname does not belong on your resume nor in job search discussions. It detracts from your professional image. Even if your nickname is seemingly innocent, such as "Skip" or "Bubba," it can still be a distraction to some interviewers who may be a little stodgy or formal. Happily, this potential stigma fades away as you gain work experience and your resume expands with accomplishments. For right now, as you begin to interview, use your given name until you are hired. Then you can let people know informally that it's OK to call you "Ace" or "Boomer." I'm sure you know the ones that will always be out of bounds.

THE COVER LETTER

An important and absolutely necessary adjunct to the resume is the cover letter. Don't send a resume out for a job that you really want without one. Why? It sets you apart from all the other candidates who fail to send one, and gives you a chance to expand on who you are in a more personal sense. Keep it short, under one hundred words.

All the information in the letter should add to, not repeat what is in your resume. Here's your chance to mention something about how you relate to the company, whether it's knowing someone who works there (very important) to mentioning an article you just read that was very favorable to the company. I promise you that whoever gets the resume will probably read the cover letter. They get so few of them that they really won't mind taking the time to do it.

YOUR INFORMATION PACKET

If getting a particular job is especially important to you, you might want to go further than the cover letter and create an information packet. When you consider how effective and creative you were in using PowerPoint or other multimedia software to create presentations while in college, why not create a presentation/marketing plan about you and blend it with the specific operations of the company that you want to be a part of? Putting this together will take a few hours work, but it might provide you with a shortcut to the front of the interviewing line. It almost certainly will.

The key ingredient of this information packet is your creativity. It should be simple, contain a maximum of four items: your resume, a cover letter, a PowerPoint CD, and a creative item to get the interviewer's attention.

GUIDELINES FOR THE INFORMATION PACKET

Your Resume

I've stressed the fact already that your resume must reflect key words found in the job description. Your key strengths must be translated into benefits the company will gain should they hire you. Showing results achieved in previous work, community involvement, and/or academe is part of this process. Getting good results means accomplishments you achieved that you can point to with pride: I'm talking about recognition of any kind for doing a great job, e.g., promotions, awards, prizes won, certificates of achievement, an article about you in the student newspaper or other media.

Your Cover Letter

The letter should be tailored specifically to the needs of the company and how your background addresses those needs. State positively and professionally that you request an interview to show how you can help them achieve their goals.

Your PowerPoint CD

Since this piece is the heart of your packet and will require some work on your part, *it should be saved for the job opportunities that are very important to you.* The creation of this piece should not be rushed, nor should it be just a rehash of your resume. This is an opportunity to enhance what you provide in the resume, to show your strengths and appropriateness for the job in images and data as well as words. After you have collected all the data you can on the company and the particular job you are vying for, let all the information bounce around in your head for 24 hours. This time gives your inventiveness a chance to develop.

Like your cover letter, the PowerPoint presentation should be short — no more than 10-12 slides (or 2 or 3 minutes if timed) — just enough time to give the interviewer/hiring manager a good idea of who you are, your relevant background, positions you held, results you have achieved, your personal values, skills, why you have chosen the career field you have, and most important, what you can do for them. It should be an expansion of the **2-Minute Bio** (coming up in Chapter 5) you prepared for answering the basic question/request that starts almost all interviews, "Who are you?" / "Tell me about yourself."

A word of caution: If you've ever seen the movie "Legally Blonde," we're not talking about an Elle Woods law school application video complete with pet chihuahua.

Use the achievements on your resume as a guide, and relate them to activities, initiatives, goals — anything that the company is currently involved in. This will make your packet timely and right to the point about what's important to them.

A Creative Item

The creative item should stand on its own and reflect your creativity as it relates to your wanting to work at that company — for instance, a business idea or solution. This will require some thought and research.

Case in Point:

A candidate I heard about through a CEO associate of mine, Gary S., dreamed for a long time about being an advertising copywriter. He came across an ad for such a position at Remington Firearms, the legendary gun manufacturer. Realizing it would be a real challenge to get an interview there, he created a simple information packet about himself and what value he would bring to Remington. He went to a target practice range, bought some paper targets, took his highest scoring target, put it in a package with his resume and cover letter, and mailed it all to a contact name he had at Remington. He got the interview.

Another candidate, a salesperson in a pharmaceutical company, wanted to change jobs but didn't know what she wanted to do. In the course of contacting people in her network, she went to a pub with a friend and met a person who, just by chance, was with a company that was hiring in sales.

After a brief friendly conversation, which included the fact that this hiring manager was an avid hockey fan (important detail!), the woman got the manager's card. The next day she created an info packet for this hiring manager which included her resume, a short cover letter reminding him of their meeting in the pub, and a creative item: the creative item was a *hockey puck* on which she had written, "Take a Shot on Me." She not only got an interview ... she got a job.

Creativity almost always gets attention, sets you apart from the competition, and goes a long way to getting you what you want.

If you can't come up with a simple but creative idea in the time frame you have to work with, enclose your **30-day plan** (discussed in Chapter 4) instead of an information packet.

If you didn't take business courses while you were in college and have had no marketing-related exposure, review any PowerPoint presentations you have created and construct a presentation about you as to how effective you would be in a particular position. Use the basic selling techniques (presented in Chapter 4), and explain how your **personal value proposition** relates to benefits for the prospective for-profit or non-profit organization; in other words, how you will help them achieve their goals as related to their mission statement and the specific job description.

As with anything you will be presenting to a prospective employer, have a member of your support group evaluate the packet before you use it.

And the Information Packet Goes To ...

The packet should be addressed to the hiring manager. If you don't know their name and can't find it out, get the name of a manager who is in the same department ... any manager other than HR (you'll hear more about why, shortly). If the company is small, any manager's name is better than none or the clichéd, anonymous "To Whom It may Concern." With a name on it, the packet will look important and will be passed on to the appropriate area person/department. Managers in most companies are responsible and will see that this is done.

Remember, your main objective in creating a compact, creative information packet is to get an interview when you otherwise couldn't. The information packet is not only an impressive first impression but can also be a notable leave-behind after a face-to-face interview. Although there is no guarantee of success in using an information packet to get an interview, it boosts your odds tremendously. Hardly anyone puts forth this kind of assertive effort, and I can tell you that it has worked for others in the past. You will be noticed, and this is one hell of a lot more innovative and distinctive of you than just broadcasting your resume all over the Internet.

PORTFOLIO OF PREVIOUS WORK

More experienced job seekers should have a portfolio of work created in previous jobs in addition to an information packet, a portfolio of non-proprietary work samples that can verify the results you claim you have achieved in your resume and in the interview. I advise you not to make this portfolio a part of your information packet because this type of information has to be explained to the interviewer if they are interested in you.

Moreover, make sure that what you present in your portfolio is appropriate to reveal to another employer and does not infringe upon the intellectual property rights of your former employer; some of this information may be close to the line of proprietary material, i.e., work that your former employer specified should not be shared outside the company, sensitive work that you produced in your former jobs and should not be left behind or placed in your personal information packet in any case. Choose general work that you can use to show that you achieved results in former positions. Again, do not share proprietary information or data from former employers with anyone. If you're not sure about what you want to use, either get permission from your previous employer or leave it out.

THE HR DEPARTMENT

Once you get your resume, cover letter and personal information packet together, be sure you don't send it to the company HR department until you have exhausted all other means to get a contact name or best, the name of the hiring manager.

Why?

The HR department has the power to say *No*, but they don't have the power to say *Yes*. HR can eliminate you as a candidate before you get to see the hiring manager, and they cannot hire you without his/her OK.

HR's number one job is to protect the company. They act as the screener for almost all incoming resumes; if someone in HR doesn't feel that your resume is what they are looking for, it goes into the round file. Also, if the resume software screener has determined that your resume doesn't have enough of the keywords found in the online job description – round file.

Picture this possible scenario: the screener is an HR staffer and not feeling well that day, and even if he sees that you are marginally qualified, because he is a Cal grad and you graduated from Stanford... well, so long, buddy. Remember, there are hundreds to thousands of resumes coming in, so the majority of HR's time is spent eliminating candidates. The hiring manager is the one that has the power to hire you, not HR.

It is also important to note that once you have gone directly to HR without having spoken to anyone else in the company, you must go through them from that point on. If, after you have spoken to HR, you go around them or over their heads to another manager, it will be seen as a serious breach of protocol and it will go badly for you. At the very least they will be highly pissed off that you dared bypass their company procedures, and they could make life difficult for you. It's in your interest to not let this happen.

Still, often you will have to go through HR because it is company policy, so buck up and do it, and do it graciously, which can ingratiate you with the HR manager. Just make sure that you stand out through a creative package, as we discussed previously.

GETTING TO THE HIRING MANAGER

By now you know that the best way to increase your chances for getting an interview with any company —by far — is to get to the hiring manager.

This can be difficult unless you have a contact within the target company, difficult because companies protect the names of managers at the operating level for a variety of reasons. It keeps them from getting distracting phones calls from customers (Customer Service is supposed to handle most of these), from competitors seeking information not available in the media, from headhunters like me who are trying to steal them away, or from anyone or anything else outside of their normal responsibilities that would keep them from doing their job.

> *TIP: Try calling at lunchtime when the regular receptionist is not there. The replacement receptionist may not be as familiar with the SOP (standard operating procedure) to screen callers and just might give you a name and put the call through for you. It is also fruitful sometimes to call in the early morning, say around 7-7:30, before the normal workday begins. Managers of all kinds frequently come in early to get work done before the day's activities start up.*

If you are lucky enough to have the hiring manager's name but can't get directly to them, ask *anyone* who answers your call to redirect you to them. If you are really lucky and have a direct extension from a business card you got at a trade show or from one of the members in your support group, you might bypass all screeners and get right to the hiring manager.

One-Minute Telephone Pitch

Before you make the attempt, however, write up and rehearse a **one-minute telephone pitch**. In this pitch you are selling YOU to the listener, i.e., a hiring manager. Some recruiters call it the "elevator pitch," which supposes you have a chance to share a short elevator ride with the hiring manager. You have a captive audience for a very short period of time; what will you say that gets their interest? Let's face it, though, how often does the elevator opportunity come up? What's far more common is the telephone encounter.

So, go to it: describe, in approximately 100 to 125 words, or what you can comfortably say in one minute, how your **personal value proposition** (your strengths and key related experience) relates to benefits for the prospective employer and how you will help them achieve their goals within the scope of the specific job description. Seems like a lot of information, which it is.

The trick is to develop your statement, hone it until it feels and sounds natural and uncanned. Try it out on someone in your support group; if they say it doesn't ring true, go back and revise it until it does. Record it on your mobile phone and play it back; critique and improve.

Now you are prepared to make the call. Although they are instructed not to do it, a receptionist, a department or team assistant might slip and give you the name of a manager in the area of the company you are interested in, if your question to them is imaginative enough.

For instance, call the targeted company's general number and get an operator or other live person (not so easy with today's automated circular telephone answering systems). Explain simply that you're trying to get to the manager that has an opening in a specific area that you believe you are qualified for. If the person is doing their job properly, they will direct you to HR, which is exactly what you don't want them to do. So quickly explain that you heard from a friend at a trade show (or whatever your source was) that there was an opening in sales, or accounting, or whatever. Would he/she know who the manager in that area might be? You might get lucky and get a name.

You might get connected to another assistant in the immediate area of the hiring manager. Ask the same question. The worst that will happen is that they will take your name and number and say that they will have someone call you back. You might get lucky again and someone other than an HR person will return your call. Now you can explain your situation with your sincere, succinct benefits-based one-minute telephone pitch. Remember, no more than one minute, or you will probably lose them.

> TIP: *If you can't get the hiring manager's name at this point, ask if you can send your information packet to the person you are speaking with. Now you have a specific name in the area or department of the company that you are interested in. Get this person's number, too, and ask them if you can call in 2 or 3 days to make sure that they got your packet. If your packet looks impressive enough, they will probably pass it on to the hiring manager.*

Now it's up to the gods again, but at the very least you got your name in the door.

When you first try this routine, expect to be at least a little intimidated. If you persist, you will get better and more polished at it and be less reluctant to do it. It may take a while, but with several attempts at various target companies, your creativity will emerge and eventually you will find some gold nuggets in the form of contact names. I promise you that you will, because I used this simple routine many, many times as a headhunter over the years and it paid off for me.

Above all, remember this: **Be persistent ... but always be gracious**.

Other resources that might provide you with contact names at the operation level in the target company, in addition to your own network, may be trade journals, archives of the local newspaper of the town or city where the company is based, your college career center, alumni associations that are willing to share networking information, the web pages of local charities and volunteer organizations and, of course, Facebook, LinkedIn and other networking sites. Put your imagination to work and find more resources.

It's a lot of work, but that's what you're looking for, isn't it: *a lot of work*. Don't kid yourself about this. As I've said before, looking for work is a full-time job in itself. If you're not putting in at least six hours a day in related job search activities, you're not doing the job you're supposed to be doing right now, until you find a better one.

CHAPTER 3

PREPARING FOR THE INTERVIEW ... AND WHAT TO DO THE NIGHT BEFORE

"You've got to be very careful if you don't know where you are going because you might not get there." (Yogi Berra)

This is the time that you do your countdown to the interview to make sure that you are fully prepared for tomorrow.

THE INTERVIEWER'S POINT OF VIEW

One of the best things you can do tonight is something that few candidates do, that is, to put yourself in the interviewer's shoes. Why? If you can understand at least a little bit about where the interviewer is coming from, you will be more successful at creating a positive approach to the interview — a game plan, if you will — about the way you will conduct yourself. You will be better able to construct questions tailored to the interviewer and, more important, be prepared to answer their questions and impress them.

For starters, do your best to get the interviewer's name in advance, especially if they are the hiring manager. If you can't get the name from HR, check to see if they are mentioned on the company website. Did you find anything about them on Google or another search engine?

Hiring is an expensive, time-consuming and even a risky business for companies. It's expensive for two reasons. First, it takes up management time that could otherwise be used for more directly-profitable purposes. Second, every day that a position remains unfilled means another day of lower productivity for the company, and if the position relates directly to the bottom line (and most do, in some fashion), less revenue coming in. The risk relates to the fact that of all hiring of college-educated people, across all industries, approximately 20% of these new hires don't work out, meaning that they are gone after a year or so. This is a discouraging figure when you consider the time and effort put in by management to select and train what they believe to have been the best candidates after multiple interviews by experienced managers.

And what does the interviewer and their company really know about you, the candidate, at this point, beyond the interview, your resume, and references? The company can't say that they really "know" you even if they have had you thoroughly vetted. In a practical sense, you, as a new employee, are going to have access to proprietary information from day one. In effect you now have the keys to the office. Most new hires are honest people, but there are always those few who aren't and they can do a lot of damage by carelessly misusing, or outright stealing company information including trade secrets. Even with the restricted access and internal security systems in place in corporations today, industrial espionage and theft are still multi-million dollar problems.

You may think that as the candidate you have the toughest assignment in the deal, but really it's the interviewer who does. They speak for the company but they also think for themselves, often weighing their company's needs against their own gut instincts about a candidate's suitability. It's a balancing act, and you may never know which face they're showing you. It's prudent for you to be aware of and respond to both perspectives.

I've found the interviewing experience for the interviewer to be at least as important as training or motivation or both when it comes to successful outcomes. However, being an intelligent, motivated expert in the area for which you are interviewing job candidates is no guarantee for a high degree of success in the *interviewing process* itself. As in most things, experience is essential for ongoing success.

From the human side of the interviewer perspective, consider the fact that interviewing is an art, not a science. It is difficult to do well. From my experience, many interviewers have had little or no formal interviewing training. Many are self-taught out of necessity, have read a "how to" interviewing book or a few articles in the media, and proceed to do the best they can.

More than a few times as a headhunter I have been surprised at the inexperience of some interviewers, based on feedback from my clients and my candidates. Knowing this is not a negative; on the contrary, it's valuable information. While you may be thinking that you have enough to focus on with your own performance, and that the interviewer's lack of experience is not your problem, think again. Consider for a moment that the interviewer might be new at it and therefore may be feeling a little anxious themselves. Consider that the interviewer may not be prepared for the interview, meaning you must be even more prepared yourself.

Let's look at this more closely.

Ask yourself: What would an experienced manager with extensive knowledge in their field, but with little interviewing expertise, do to alleviate their jitters and yet be effective?

I once asked an experienced senior manager who had no formal training in the interview process this question. His answer provides a solid framework for interviewing:

"After reviewing the candidate's background," he explained, "I ask myself three questions:

1) *Has the candidate, even a young one without much experience, demonstrated the ability to get things from point 'A' to point 'B' successfully?*

2) *Do they have specific knowledge or experience in the job area in question?*

3) *Do they have a passion for what they do?*

The manager concluded, "If I can get two out of three of these, the candidate just became a finalist. If I get all three, I'll probably make an offer."

As to the first question, has this candidate been successful at what they have done so far? Have they shown that they can get results at whatever it is they have done in the past? Earning a college degree or a tradesman accreditation certainly counts for this kind of success and it's one of the reasons that having a degree is such a big deal for young job searchers.

Question two deals directly with the fact that specific knowledge and successful experience in your field of endeavor are extremely important in getting a new job. Education provides the foundation for your success, and experience gained over the years increases your value as you move along your career path, becoming more valuable with each passing year. After your second successful job, education becomes a smaller factor in the candidate evaluation process, but it will always be an essential qualifying criterion.

The third question about having a passion for what you do is valuable to companies because it means that you are driven to do your best. When you do your best, the company wins because you are making them better at what they do. In a way, your passion makes it seem to them that they are getting a little extra for their money. Being passionate about your work doesn't mean showing up to work foaming at the mouth or running down the company hallways with your hair on fire. It means operating in a measured, intelligent, cooperative, sustainable approach that *goes beyond expectations.*

Case in Point:

As an undergraduate at the University of Illinois, I was a member of the Evans Scholars fraternity. A trustee of the Evans Scholars Foundation, a wealthy and highly successful businessman, came down to Champaign-Urbana from Chicago to speak to us about graduation and getting that first job and *keeping* it. He told us that, when everything else was equal among job candidates and those in line for promotion, the thing he looked for most was that quality that makes people ask to do more than what is expected of them: Passion.

If you are an inexperienced job applicant, this could mean being an officer in a campus club, volunteering at a local non-profit, or perhaps summer work, doing some kind of community-focused service. There are lots of opportunities to help you go beyond expectations and stand out. And they look great on a resume.

If you're already in your first or second job, it means assisting other employees with problems not in your immediate area of responsibility when you have the time, or if you make the time by staying after hours. If you make sure in a subtle way that important people know that you are doing this, your chances of getting promoted go way up.

You'll hear these statements a lot in your career: "That's not my job" and "It's not my responsibility." Do yourself a favor and never utter either one. These are promotion killers and will make you look bad in an interview or performance review.

Referencing the three questions in your response to the interviewer's standard opening statement, "Tell me about yourself," gives you a focus and helps to put both you and a newer (and possibly anxious) interviewer at ease.

Another way to help the interviewer feel more secure about you is to describe how hiring you will make them look good to their boss.

Chances are that as an entry-level candidate you will be interviewed by a junior to mid-level hiring manager, or what we headhunters call a one- or two-mistake guy. If they are young and inexperienced at interviewing, they will be allowed one or two mistakes regarding candidates they hire that don't work out. The interviewer is very aware that if they hire you and you don't work out and are soon gone, they will look very bad to their boss. Depending on how badly the new hire screwed up in the job, the interviewer could be assigned a lesser role in interviewing candidates in the future. If they make three such mistakes within a year or two of each other, they may be pulled from interviewing altogether or be reduced to a perfunctory role, for appearances only. Someone else will make the hiring decisions for them and new hires they did not choose themselves will be forced upon them whether they like it or not. This does not make for a happy, productive situation.

What's Going On in the Interviewer's Head?

Your objective is to get to the hiring manager, the one who makes the final decision, and that means connecting as well as you can with the intermediate interviewer. One way to address this problem and help put the interviewer at ease during the early stages of the interview is to find out what's important to them and then to listen carefully. If you can figure out what they want out of this position early on in the interview, you're halfway home.

I'm not talking about the obvious stuff, such as being a reliable, honest, capable person with the basic skill set who will show up when you're supposed to. The person that gets the job will show that they bring much more than this. You must also show that you are an over-achiever, that you are easy to motivate, relatively easy to manage, that you fit into the company culture, are not a pain-in-the-ass most of the time, and otherwise make life easier for the hiring manager.

Now show them how you can address the issues they just raised. Will you help them do their job, or won't you? Can you help them look better at what they do or can't you? By the end of the interview, if you can't clearly communicate how you will help them do their job better and make them look good, you will not get an offer. Period.

Later in your career when you are interviewed by a higher-level hiring manager, (a four- or more-mistake guy), the principle of making the interviewer feel confident in you still applies. Once again, you must help them substantiate to their boss why they hired you and why it was a good decision for the company. You do this by explaining your **personal value proposition** — linking your strengths and skills to benefits that the company will realize that will make it prosper and make your potential boss look good. In Chapter 4, when we analyze salesmanship and your basic value proposition, I'll show you how to do this.

SOFT SKILLS

Throughout the interview, the interviewer will be looking for something special in the candidate. These "soft skills" are the intangibles of our personality and experience that are hard to define, that go beyond training or education but are essential to succeeding professionally. They are learned by living and growing through experience.

All good interviewers will be on the lookout for these soft skills qualities:

- **The ability to communicate well**. *Does the candidate listen well and articulate ideas in speech and in writing that others understand?*

- **The ability to persuade**. *Can the candidate not only communicate well but also convince others to do what needs to be done?*

- **The ability to motivate**. *Once ideas have been communicated well and others are persuaded to a specific point of view, can the candidate energize them to take effective action?*

- **Creative ability.** *Will the candidate have the ability to "think outside the box" and come up with new ideas that will help the company be a better, more profitable, more efficient place than it was before they were hired? Can they solve everyday problems related to company business?*

- **The ability to think on one's feet.** *Can the candidate come up with a sound, informed answer to a question with an on-the-spot answer? Likewise, can they respond to a situation under pressure with an effective course of action?*

- **Effective interpersonal skills.** *Can the candidate build trust in co-workers or subordinates? Are they reasonably pleasant to get along with? Can they express empathy with fellow employees, and provide wisdom and guidance when appropriate?*

- **Good chemistry.** *Will the candidate have the ability to establish a positive, energetic working relationship with customers and fellow employees?*

- **The ability to organize.** *Can the candidate effectively manage people, things, or both, to solve the company's problems and achieve results as stated in the company mission statement?*

- **The ability to fit into the company culture.** *Does the candidate have the kind of personality that melds well with the company personality?*

Of the nine soft skills mentioned above, the most important to interviewers, in my experience, are **communication skills** and **creativity**. However, the above list is not necessarily exhaustive. Enumerating and defining "soft skills" is akin to defining anyone's personality, a daunting task to be sure. But the list gives you a good idea of what the interviewer is looking for beyond the official job description.

THE BASIC REASON WHY COMPANIES WANT TO HIRE YOU

They have a problem, and you are about to make clear to them why you are the solution.

First off, you're a college graduate (or about to become one). Why is it that companies insist that you must have a college degree to be hired for certain positions? It is policy at most companies, a rule established by senior management. To get an exception to policy, a junior level manager would have to go to senior management to get an OK.

What's the number one reason that companies insist on hiring degreed candidates for certain positions? When I have asked this question of my students over several years, not one of them has been able to give the answer that I was looking for. Not one. These very bright people gave answers that you typically read in the media, such as, "Companies insist on hiring college graduates because they are: intelligent, resourceful, persistent, disciplined, the best and the brightest of their generation, dependable, reliable, creative ..." plus a few more adjectives which escape me right now. All of these descriptions are correct for the most part, but not what I was looking for.

The main reason that companies insist on hiring college graduates for certain jobs is this: **Profitability**. How can the company profit by hiring you? They are convinced that you can help them solve problems, lessen expenses, improve operations. Bottom line: **YOU CAN HELP THEM MAKE MONEY and/or SAVE MONEY.**

Don't ever forget this.

*If you are in sales, bringing in revenue or helping your company's customers stay happy, you are helping your company **make money**.* What happy customers provide is repeat business, and repeat business is the heart of company success.

If you are interviewing for a position that does not help a company make money directly, *you have to show in your personal value proposition that you will help them save money*. Whether you are an employee that helps make money directly, as in sales, or by helping to get repeat business, or an employee that helps save money by increasing company productivity and efficiency internally, it doesn't really matter. You will all meet happily at the company's bottom line.

Every time I made these statements in the classroom, there was stunned silence. What these students were feeling at the time, I believe, was what we all feel when a simple truth that we have been living with for some time is pointed out to us. It's the recognition of the obvious that wasn't obvious just a few minutes ago. The vast majority of them never have had specific profit and loss responsibility. Very few of them have had a career level job at this point in their lives.

No one ever challenged the statement once they heard it. They accepted it immediately.

I want to stress that for-profit companies aren't charities, social clubs, fraternities, or sororities. They don't have the power of taxation, grants, or private donations to bail them out if something bad happens financially.

For small companies, especially, credit markets will likely be tight for years into the future, as our nation goes through an extensive economic restructuring. Instead of being able to borrow money to help them survive, they now have to find the money themselves by increasing sales. Four out of five new companies fail within the first five years of their existence. In 2011 alone there were almost 50,000 business bankruptcies. So making money has to be their first concern, especially as evidenced after the financial crisis of 2008. Showing a small company how you can help them make money by converting your strengths into specific benefits to them will not only get their attention, but will also probably get you a job.

In large companies the need for making money is also paramount, but the measuring schema is different. Depending on how distant your job or function is from the corporate bottom line, the hiring manager will be more interested in how you can help them solve problems or achieve objectives that they are measured on. These can be:

- A percent of sales quota they need to attain

- How quickly and efficiently they successfully complete projects

- How efficient their supply chain is

- Lowering their departmental overhead

- Making their channels of distribution more timely, efficient and less costly

- In a large corporation there are many functions such as these that are measured in specific terms. All of these measurements or objectives are directly related to the corporation making money, increasing earnings, and getting the stock price up. If these things happen it will mean, in most cases, that the boss will get a bonus or a raise and make more money. In for-profit companies it always it comes down to making money. Always.

Sometimes a hiring manager will have a hidden agenda — maybe they have been ordered to hire a candidate from an under-represented group in order to improve their company image, or they want to hire someone who has the basic qualifications but will not be a threat to them (i.e., taking over their job at some point). In the end, if the person hired doesn't help the hiring manager make money for the company or doesn't help to advance the manager's overall performance, both the hiring manager and the underperforming candidate will be history in the not too distant future.

Making money for a commercial company in legal, ethically sound ways is a good thing, a critical thing. It enables companies to hire millions of people and to provide them with the means to have a chance at finding stability and a good life. Without it, companies wouldn't be around to make billions of dollars in charitable donations through their foundations, or to provide products that save lives, or make life a lot easier for all of us. Don't think of the pursuit of money as a cold, selfish thing. It only becomes that if it's your one and only pursuit.

Let me state again that the main reason that companies insist on hiring college graduates and other degreed or certified individuals is that from past experience they know that these people **will help them make money, save money,** or **raise money**.

THE NON-PROFIT WORLD AND MONEY

*In the non-profit world **raising money**, not making money, is the important thing.* Non-profit means just that. However, non-profits are constantly trying to raise money from donations, federal grants, or from their states, cities and counties. At the end of the year the IRS checks up on them to make sure that there are no excess funds remaining on the books. Non-profits essentially must break even and have a zero balance on their books, even if it means giving away any surplus that they can't spend responsibly to accomplish their mission.

So, the need for money in the non-profit world is as crucial for existence as it is in the for-profit world. However, if you are not interviewing for a job in the development department of the non-profit, the ability to manage money remains in the background (sometimes way, way in the background) and other things come to the fore during the interview process, such as: your level of education and academic pedigree, experience with other non-profits (sometimes even dissimilar non-profits will do); and most important, whom you know (which unfortunately has given non-profits the reputation of cronyism).

I'm not trying to discourage you if your quest is for a job in the non-profit world. Lots of excellent, critical work is done there by front-line troops such as teachers, nurses, doctors, police, counselors and volunteers. But after working for and volunteering in non-profit institutions for more than fourteen years, my experience is that these institutions are very different from their for-profit counterparts and, by logical deduction, so is the job interview process. There's a different set of rules, requirements and standards in non-profits from for-profits, essentially a different reality.

An in-depth discussion of the non-profit job interview process goes beyond the scope of this book. My advice before interviewing at a non-profit is to ask them directly what they are looking for in a candidate for a specific position. Formulate your benefit statements around this and keep things simple. Most important: *Try to connect with someone in the non-profit area who can advise you and who might help sway things your way.*

THE IMPORTANCE OF REHEARSING

If you haven't done it yet, especially if you are in the early stages of interviewing, you must *rehearse*. You would never consider jumping into the ocean without first having practiced in a pool, would you? Interviewing is no different. Don't drown yourself — if you don't rehearse, not only will you blow your chances for serious consideration but you risk embarrassment for not being prepared.

Rehearsing not only builds confidence, it also makes you think more clearly and inevitably something will occur to you during the rehearsal process that you hadn't thought of before. You have researched the company until your eyes bled and you have six or seven intelligent questions to ask (described at the end of this chapter). Additional questions to ask the interviewer will frequently occur to you during the rehearsal process.

Even though you will get better with each interview, if you continue to give it your best effort, it may occur to you at some point that you've got this down now and you really don't need to rehearse any more. Don't kid yourself. If you think that the next interview is a gimme, you're setting yourself up for a fall. Even experienced public speakers such as corporate CEOs and politicians have been known to mess up an important presentation because it was obvious that they hadn't prepared or rehearsed.

I recently asked two recruiter associates in the Bay Area about the most serious mistakes that candidates make during the interview process today. Byron C. is a young recruiter with two years experience in the finance and accounting area. Joe L., is a twenty-five year headhunter veteran and personal friend in the high-tech arena. *Both said that the biggest blunder that candidates make today is not being prepared.* As you will remember from the Job Fair section in the Preview and Appendix E, this was the number-one reason cited by interviewers as to why interviewees fail.

The best way to find out if you are prepared to interview is to rehearse with a friend(s) from your support group. The second best way to find out is after the interview. Did you get an offer or didn't you? Did you get a "next step" or not?

MOCK INTERVIEWS

Recording a mock interview in advance of the real thing and reviewing it with a member(s) of your support group is like getting to see a sneak preview of a new movie. All good sales training programs do mock interviews between prospect and salesperson because they allow you to figuratively step outside of yourself and see how you perform under pressure.

What pressure, you ask? This is a closed session with other professional people you know, and it's a controlled situation. There's nothing to lose here, right?

The hell there isn't.

Performing in front of your peers while being recorded and knowing that you will face a critique afterward from both trainers and peers is one of the most stressful situations you can face in your entire business career. The pressure to perform is extreme. After going through this experience, many of my sales compatriots at Xerox felt that the *real sales calls were a lot easier*. I agree completely. Great sales training programs put their employees through this ordeal because the insights and skills gained are invaluable and part of the basis of successful sales careers ... and, by extension, a means to successful interviewing.

The purpose of recorded mock interview sessions is to build confidence in personal encounters, to help provide a basis for thinking on one's feet, and to provide a profile of you that can be used to correct or improve upon personal mannerisms and behaviors in the interview (or sales) situation. These mock sessions provide help with matters such as the initial greeting, handshakes, general appearance, eye contact, voice level, posture, and your delivery skills.

Most important, this role-playing allows you to see how you, the interviewee, manage both asking and answering questions. Listening well is vitally important, too, not only to forming strong, intelligent answers, but also to show the prospect/interviewer how important this interview is to you, and how well prepared you are.

As you observe your strong and weak points during the replay of your mock performance you are engaging in a critique of your interviewing style, at least the way it is now. Are you talking too much (or too little), not smiling enough? Are you speaking clearly or are you hard to understand? Is there a general feeling that you are on the defensive, as opposed to being your usual self and more outgoing than not? Has a support group member asked you a tough question or two that you were not aware of in advance? How did you answer? Were you convincing? What changes do your support group friends suggest that you make?

Don't be reluctant to ask for feedback and criticism: it's the safest place to get valuable, trusted advice, even though it may sting a little to hear what they have to say. A real interviewer will rarely give you genuine feedback about your style or how you answered questions ... unless they hire you.

Now you can make changes to your presentation style, be much better prepared for the real thing, and gain another advantage over your competition.

THE IMPORTANCE OF FIRST IMPRESSIONS

When preparing for the interview the night before, you must give serious consideration to your appearance and your demeanor. For good or bad, humans are prejudiced animals. Because of this, we all make judgments about a person the minute we set eyes upon them. How you are sized up initially will have a very important influence on the ultimate results of the encounter.

The idea here is to have as many favorable things about you as possible presented to the person you're looking at and conversely, as few negative things as possible. The phrase used in the recruiting business to describe negative factors about you is *negative disqualifiers.* Many of these disqualifiers, meaning factors going against you that will eliminate you as a candidate, are evident in the first five minutes of an encounter. These are the obvious things that are noticed immediately by a recruiter or interviewer ... that is to say, things that are obvious to the recruiter, but may not be obvious to you.

Negative disqualifiers that stand out: chewing gum during a business conversation; wearing stained or sloppy clothing; talking way too loud or conversely, mumbling; interrupting the interviewer when he/she is talking. More subtle elements that may not be obvious to young people who have just graduated from a liberal, open culture are things such as visible tattoos, lots of body piercing jewelry, haircuts outside of the everyday norm of the business world, dress that is way, way too casual for the occasion, poor posture, a weak handshake, bad breath, use of slang, poor grammar, poor manners.

These are negatives that can disqualify a candidate, depending upon the amount of contact they would be expected to have with the client's customers, and the dress code and code of conduct of the interviewing company. One thing an interviewer will be thinking for sure is, "How will this person look to my customers?"

As you prepare for the interview the night before, eliminate as many distractions to the "sale" you will be trying to make the next day. When in doubt, hide the tattoo(s), take all but very small, simple jewelry off altogether, avoid wearing perfume or cologne, and dress more formally than not.

You will never be criticized or looked down upon if men dress in a suit and tie, or women wear similar business attire. There are rules in the business club that you must now follow if you want to become a member. It may be that after you get hired you may dress and act much more informally according to the company culture, but not now. Once again, **ANYTHING** that could distract the interviewer from the task at hand, such as loud clothing or poor grooming, should be avoided.

Can you fail to establish a strong initial impression and still have a successful interview? Yes, but it's not easy. No competent interviewer will eliminate a candidate based upon five minutes of contact, especially if you have been pre-screened and your credentials are strong unless there has been a terrible faux pas or gross behavior of some kind during the interview. Why take a chance and get strike two on you just after you step into the batter's box? Again, eliminate anything that could be considered a distraction.

> *TIP: If you are still in doubt about your appearance after you have asked trusted friends or family in your support group, go to the company in question the day before if you can, and observe how people look as they come and go at lunch time or when they leave at the end of the day.*

CHECKLISTS

Checklists can be helpful, especially the night before an important interview. However, checklists can be hazardous if they are extensive and you feel you must memorize them. I'm referring specifically to long lists of "commonly asked questions." Recalling items from a long list or checklist when under pressure can put you at a distinct disadvantage if your recall isn't really good. Airline pilots don't trust to memory alone but always use a *short* checklist prior to takeoff. So should you.

Final Prep Checklist

1. What are your objectives for this interview?

- To determine if you want to work for this company?

- To close for a next step?

- To close for a job offer?

- To gather information only?

- To improve your interviewing skills only (informational interview)?

2. What will be your personal calming thought as you wait for the interview?

3. Have you reviewed the Basic Four Questions? (Ch. 5) Remember, these four questions will always be asked in some format.

4. Have you reviewed the general questions that might be asked by the interviewer? (Ch. 5)

5. Do you have your questions prepared for the interviewer? (Ch. 5)

6. Is your information packet ready to go? (Ch. 2 & 4)

- Cover Letter

- Resume (2 copies)

- PowerPoint CD

- A creative item

- A portfolio of your past work

- Your 30-Day Plan (2 copies)

7. Do you have two "small talk" ideas ready to start out the interview? If you know the name of the interviewer/hiring manager, have you found anything about them on the company website? Have you Googled them? Great ideas for "small talk" can come from these sources.

8. Have you written out your personal value proposition as it relates specifically to this company and the posted job description? (Ch. 4)

9. Have you rehearsed your 2-Minute Bio (Ch. 5), preferably in front of a support group member, but at least in front of a mirror?

10. Do you have answers prepared for behavioral questions that relate to important results that you produced in the past in school or on the job? A personalized vignette related to your best strengths, that is, results you pro-

duced in the past, will impress the interviewer, help them remember you, and possibly give you a leg up on your competition. It works.

11. Have your social media sites been cleaned up? If not, have you created a shadow social website with a different email address for professional use only? This is one way of protecting your privacy without killing yourself as relates to the world of work. (App. C) Have you notified your references that they might be getting a call? (Ch. 7)

12. Have you reviewed your basic sales techniques, i.e., your ability to sell yourself? (Ch. 4) If you want the job, are you prepared to "Close 'em"? (This means asking for the job.) Examples: *"Mr. Smith, after researching your company, and after our excellent interview today, I want you to know that I want this job."* Or, *"After the research I have done on your company, and after our excellent discussion about this job today, I want to tell you that I am convinced that I can do this job. Do you feel the same way?"*

13. If things start to go bad at any point in the interview, what are you prepared to do? See Ch. 8, "What if ... things start to go bad in the interview?"

14. Appearance & miscellaneous:

- Have you given yourself enough time to get to the interview with 15 minutes to spare? Do you have exact directions, a street address, and an office number? Don't leave home without them.

- Have you done a mirror check of your appearance, including clothes, shoes, hair, tattoos, excess jewelry? As far as jewelry goes, keep it simple. *Very simple.* Dress as if you are going to your brother or sister's wedding. Guys, this means a suit and tie. No excuses.

- Do you have a pocket mouth spray, and a handkerchief in case your hands start to sweat? You haven't used perfume or cologne, have you? Remember, unusual things of any kind will distract the interviewer and work against you.

- Do you have a professional-looking notebook and pen to take notes?

- Do you have at least two extra copies of your resume, and the company job description?

15. Have you done an **attitude check**? That is, are you confident, have good energy, and open to **listening** to what the interviewer has to say? Are you in a positive frame of mind and will you always explain your answers in a positive way, even when asked a negative question?

Add more items that are important to you.

Fill out your **Final Prep Checklist/Interviewing Action Plan** in this book as completely as you can. Done? Now you are as prepared as you can be and you will sleep well.

FINAL PREP CHECKLIST & INTERVIEWING ACTION PLAN

1. My objectives for this interview/this company:

_____

_____

_____

_____

2. My personal calming thought while waiting for the interview:

_____

_____

_____

_____

3. The Basic Four Questions and my general responses:

_____

_____

_____

_____

4. General questions the interviewer might ask:

_____

_____

_____

_____

5. Questions I may ask the interviewer:

_____

_____

_____

_____

6. My Information Packet & Resource Materials:

My Cover Letter –

_____

_____

_____

_____

My Resume –

_____

_____

_____

_____

My PowerPoint CD –

_____

_____

_____

_____

My Creative Item –

_____

_____

_____

_____

My portfolio of past work –

_____

_____

_____

_____

My 30-Day Plan –

_____

_____

_____

_____

7. Two "small talk" ideas to start out the interview:

_____

_____

_____

_____

8. My Personal Value Proposition as it relates specifically to this company and the posted job description:

_____

_____

_____

_____

9. My 2-Minute Bio:

_____

_____

_____

_____

10. My answers for behavioral questions relating to results that I produced in the past:

_____

_____

_____

_____

11. My social media sites (cleaned up) and references (notified):

_____

_____

_____

_____

12. My basic sales techniques & asking for the job:

_____

_____

_____

_____

13. What I can do if things start to go bad in the interview:

_____

_____

_____

_____

14. My Appearance:

_____

_____

_____

_____

15. My Attitude:

_____

_____

_____

_____

CHAPTER 4
THE HEART OF IT ALL – THE INTERVIEW ITSELF

"The person who gets the farthest is generally the one who is willing to do and dare. The 'sure-thing' boat never gets far from the shore."
(Dale Carnegie)

THE VARIABLE NATURE OF THE INTERVIEW

The interview is the heart of the job search process. All of your efforts up to this point culminate here: you either get the job or you don't.

It's a place and an experience of opposites: Here's where you must be at your best and sell yourself, all by yourself, where you must deal with the feeling of being alone (even your support group can't be with you now); where being qualified for the job may not be enough to get the job; where you have to bring everything you are as a person together, everything you have learned and rehearsed together and yet, where you don't know what's in the interviewer's script; where you are at once secure in knowing yourself yet are vulnerable because of what you don't know; and finally, where you can be on top of the world or get seriously hurt emotionally (second only to being fired).

Fear of failure is at its highest.

It's also a place of great personal victory.

Your objective is to get a job offer, and you should do everything within legal and ethical bounds to get one. You can always change your mind later if you get an offer and decide that the job is not for you after all. Without an offer, however, you have nothing.

In my experience, the typical interview process usually consists of four interviews. Google, possibly the most interviewed company in America (they get about 3,000 job applications per day),[8] follows the four-interview process.

These are the company players in one or more of these four interviews:

- A screener (usually an HR person)
- The hiring manager
- Would-be peers
- Other managers (in smaller companies, possibly the company president)

The first interview is a screening process, wherein the interviewer (who may be the hiring manager but more likely someone from HR) determines if you are basically qualified for the position. My friend Professor Joe S. calls it "passing the 'sniff' test" — if you pass, you will, hopefully, get a nod to proceed to the next step.

Interviews two and three, often conducted by the hiring manager or someone from the manager's department, get into the details of what the company is looking for in terms of specific qualifications, related experience, and how well the candidate fits the company culture. The final interview — with the hiring manager and possibly the manager's boss — will usually get down to two or three finalists.

The whole setup of the interview is an artificial one in many respects. For one, you can't actually show the interviewer that you can do the job until you have had some training, even if this is not your first job. Instead, you must go through a process of questioning that gives the company enough information on your past education and experience that will convince them that you can do it. But even with all of that, they can't be completely sure that you're "the one." All you can do is be well prepared and do the best you can in the moment.

---

8   Buck, Claudia. "YouTube Jobs Sought After, Savored." McClatchy News Service, 16 Sept. 2011.

And that could still go either way: A candidate could be very skilled at interviewing and even get the job but not be very good at actually performing in the job. Or a candidate might be highly qualified but not interview well (e.g., a reticent, analytic personality) and thus not get the job. As a headhunter I have witnessed both.

There may be times when you get interviewed for a job that has already been filled but the company still puts you through the process because the interviewer has a quota of interviews to fill that day or they just might be fishing for future candidates. Nonetheless, it can be very discouraging after you thought you had a bang-up interview and later your phone calls are not returned.

You are in the middle of a contest of elimination. Selecting the best candidate(s) necessarily means that several others must be selected out. When you report for work after you're hired, the artificial world of the interview ends, and you can concentrate on doing a great job. Elimination time is over.

One more factor that sets you up in an unpredictable, artificial situation is the undercover prejudice of the interviewer. The prejudice may exist in the interviewer alone or in the company, although prejudice on the part of the company is much harder to detect.

The following examples of prejudice are so common as to have become stereotypical: Attractive people are more likely to get hired than unattractive people; younger people are more likely to be hired than older people in many situations; lighter-skinned people more than darker-skinned; those who are thin over those who are overweight; males more than females; those who have connections versus those who don't. (Or vice versa, for reasons known only to the interviewer and/or the company.)

The most prevalent of these biases, by far, is age discrimination. If you are young and inexperienced you will face it; if you appear to be too old, you will feel it. There seems to be a narrow band of favorable ages in business that works in a candidate's favor. It starts at about age 25, assuming two or three years of successful experience, and ends at about age 40 or so, again depending upon successful experience. Age discrimination affects just about any group you can think of.

In most situations, as I mentioned before, these hiring biases and discrimination in terms of gender, race, sexual orientation, or religious affiliation are illegal but are hard to prove unless they are overtly expressed or demonstrated by the interviewer. You may never know the nature of the bias, so shoot only and always for what should be the only reason a candidate gets hired: qualifications.

So, now that I've probably depressed you with some of the real world facts about the nature of the interview (a necessary exercise to alert you to some of the uncontrollable aspects of the job search), let's focus on things you *can* control. What follows in this chapter will help you get seasoned faster as an interviewee, help you avoid some common and some not-so-common mistakes and improve your odds of winning over your competition.

HOW TO BECOME AN EFFECTIVE SALES PERSON … OF YOU

It's apparent that you will enter the interview process with at least one or two of the aforementioned uncontrollable monkeys on your back.

What can you do about it?

You can become an effective seller of *you, yourself,* and all that *you* bring to the table.

You don't have to be a great sales person, but you must train yourself to be an effective salesperson of *you.* Most people don't think that they can sell, but in fact we all have done it. You were selling from the first moment you cried as a baby to get your mother's attention and you have been in the real process of persuading people to your point of view all of your life … and in that sense you are an expert in the process and an expert in *You.* Use that self-knowledge in the practical process of selling yourself in the interview. There is power in this, and *you have the added benefit that you don't have to rehearse to be yourself.*

Start to think of yourself as a salesperson right now.

CHARACTERISTICS OF A SUCCESSFUL SALES PERSON

First, the basics. A sales person is someone who is directly responsible for a quota of some kind: selling things, services, and sometimes, as in your case, concepts/ideas. They bring revenue to a company during a defined time frame in the for-profit world.

A sales person has an assigned quota. Quotas make people directly responsible for selling something; there's a big difference between having a quota and just trying to sell something without being responsible for making the sale. Their number one goal, bar none, in the world of profit, is to get an order. They run their territory as if it is their own business and are responsible for everything that goes on there as it affects their company.

A real sales person is a problem solver, not just an order-taker. This means being creative, an out-of-the-box thinker, not just a clerk behind a counter. *Successful sales people are good listeners because it is in listening to what the customer/client has to say that they get the information to create the benefits that sell*, i.e., explaining features of a product or service in terms of benefits to the customer/client.

A good sales person has a good attitude about what they do. This translates into an enthusiasm that is infectious in the sales situation and results in getting a sale more often than their competition does.

A good sales person is persistent. They're constantly learning and are capable of bouncing back quickly after they experience rejection. Their desire is very strong. They don't just want to win, they *have* to win.

The four key components of a successful sales call are the same ones of a successful job search: desire, preparation and persistence and, above all, **attitude**. All good sales people are well prepared for the sales call/interview.

<u>**You are a real sales person, too!**</u>

This is not you, you say? The hell it isn't. Let's review the above characteristics.

- ✓ You have a personal quota and that quota is to get the job you want. You are the only one responsible for that.

- ✓ Your territory is the one you mapped out when you chose your target companies to interview.

- ✓ Your number one goal is to get a job offer. A job offer is an order, a *very big* order.

✓ You are responsible for and in charge of your own business. It's you, and you elected yourself President and CEO of Y.O.U. If you aren't responsible for you, who is?

✓ You are a problem solver. If you weren't, you wouldn't have that degree. You don't get a degree by just showing up for four or five years and just taking orders like a clerk.

✓ Creativity? Remember the creativity you used in writing all of those papers you slaved over? Yes, you're creative.

✓ You learned to listen well in class and lecture hall, where you gathered a lot of information and presumably did well on exams. Your professors understood the benefits you sold them in the form of the answers they were looking for on exams, and gave you the order — a good grade.

✓ You were well prepared for completing the demanding work required for graduation or you wouldn't have graduated, or be about to graduate.

✓ You have a great attitude about what you just accomplished, and you were persistent in getting your degree ... so good, in fact, that you were just admitted to the 33% Club. *You are now a member of an exclusive 33% minority of American adults with a college degree.* Once you're a member, you're a member for life. No one can ever take that away from you.

✓ You didn't just want to win, you *did* win.

SELLING TECHNIQUES

Now it's time to enhance your already significant selling skills by showing you some basic sales techniques you can use during the interview. We'll use a method that I was taught years ago when I first joined the sales force at Xerox Corporation. This method helped turn me into a very accomplished sales rep and it is a selling procedure that forms the basis of many selling technique books and courses today.

The number one objective of the selling process, as I have stated previously, is to get the order. The number two objective is to get the order. The number three objective is to ... **GET THE DAMN ORDER.**

I just wanted to make sure you got the idea.

To get the order, the most important thing you can do is to explain what benefits you bring to the customer/client, and describe them in language and ideas that they understand clearly and personally.

Don't confuse benefits with features about the product, the service, or yourself. **Features** are attributes and facts about you; for instance: you are female, 22 years old, have a college degree; you are intelligent, persistent, reliable and you have certain specific accomplishments as stated on your resume. Some of these features/attributes are more important than others, so from now on I'll call the important ones **strengths**.

Benefits are those attributes that take strengths about you and present them in a way that explains how you can help the client company make money, raise money, or save money. Here are some examples:

- *You managed a team of employees as an intern last summer and helped improve the efficiency of their work, which led to an increase in profits for their department.*

- *In your first job, you were put in charge of a project that was designed by you to lower the firm's overhead while increasing the level of service to a particular client.*

- *You served as an officer in the University Accounting Forum and helped increase membership by inviting managers from local companies to speak at various meetings.*

- *You worked as a volunteer while you were a student and helped a local non-profit raise money for achieving its mission.*

- In each example, you got results. ***Results you produced in the past are your best strengths.*** Where do you look for these results? They can be found in all or any of the following:

- A job you currently have

- A job you had in the past

- An internship you have now or had at one time

- A non-profit where you were a volunteer

- Campus clubs, sororities, fraternities where you held office or led a project
- Major class projects
- The grades you received, especially in difficult subjects

Results show that you have management skills/problem-solving skills and when you **convert these strengths into benefits** to the company you are interviewing with, the interviewer becomes convinced that you can help them be successful. Companies will hire you as a problem-solver who can produce results ... results that lead them directly to making, or raising, or saving money.

You get the idea. It's not strengths alone that sell — it's benefits. **Strengths** describe you and the results you got in the past. **Benefits** are how the company will profit by these strengths and thus what ultimately **sells *you* to them**.

Your **Personal Value Proposition** (PVP) is the summary of your best strengths, explained in terms of benefits to the company. Your PVP is what makes you uniquely important to interviewers, explains your worth and usefulness to them in ways that they understand and that relate to their bottom line.

Remember this: One of the most important ideas that you can take away from this book is creating your personal plan for interviewing success based upon your PVP.

When you are asked one of the Basic Four Questions, which are asked in every interview, e.g., "Tell me about yourself," it's a great time to provide a benefit statement to the interviewer. This is the first step in the basic sales techniques process.

As we'll discuss later in Chapter 5, after giving your **2-Minute Bio**, say something that relates a benefit to them. For example, you might explain that you are knowledgeable about their organization: *"Mr. Smith, I have studied your company for the past four years in college as a business major. I am familiar with the great job your company does and the success it has had. I'm sure that after reading the job description for this position I can help you continue the great work you are already known for."*

This benefit statement is very general and it is meant to be, because now you have something to build upon. Create a benefit statement that relates to your experience and *how* you can help them.

Your best ammunition for building your benefits case will come from the interviewer. This is why you must *listen carefully* to what they have to say. They will tell you what they are looking for. Then you can respond with meaningful questions and precise comments.

Effective listening is critical in selling and in interviewing. And yet, in this fast-paced digital world it seems to me that effective listening is becoming more of a lost art. Multi-tasking is the norm now and concentration and performance suffer as a result.

A recent study on multi-tasking and concentration conducted at Stanford University seems to bear this out. "After putting about 100 students through a series of three tests (on multi-tasking) researchers realized that the heavy media multi-taskers are paying a big mental price. The heavy multi-taskers consistently underperformed..."[9] Other studies have shown that before being tested, high multi-taskers were convinced that they were performing at a high-efficiency, low-error rate. Test results showed that they were not. (See more on this in Appendix C.)

Multi-tasking, such as trying to think of what you are going to say next in an interview instead of listening, can be deadly. As an example, a client of mine who had just interviewed one of my candidates told me after the interview that the candidate failed to answer the first question properly. The interviewer had to ask it again. The candidate didn't get the job. When in the interview, concentrate on the task at hand and... **LISTEN CAREFULLY!**

Proof Sources

Effective sales people use **proof sources** when they need to in order to back up a benefit statement they have just made, e.g., *"I have a reference available who will be glad to tell you what I did for them in the area of customer relations."* A proof source can be used at any time during the interview to reinforce a statement you have just made.

---

9   Gorlick, Adam. "Media multitaskers pay mental price, Stanford study shows." Stanford Report, 24 Aug. 2009.

Handling Objections

Successful sales people know how to handle **objections**. In sales, an objection is a statement made or a question raised by the customer that expresses doubt or concern. This can happen at any time during an interview, too. The interviewer may say, *"Well, Joan, this interview has gone very well, and you have a lot to recommend you for this job, but I may be looking for someone with a little more experience."*

Now is the time to assure them that although you have little experience, you're convinced that you can do the job and why. *Now* is the time you restate all the benefits that you presented earlier in the interview, and get agreement that they were important to the interviewer: *"Mr. Jones, we agreed earlier that my experience as an elected officer of the university marketing club, along with my success as an intern at ABC company, and the management skills I gained while working as a volunteer at Save the Salamanders Foundation, put me in a position for your serious consideration. I want to make it clear to you that* **I WANT THIS JOB.***"*

ASK FOR THE JOB!!!

You have stated clearly and in a respectful manner that there is no doubt in your mind that this is the job for you. The interviewer needs to hear this in order to be sure about how you feel about this job. I'll explain in the next chapter with a personal, painful example of what can happen that if you don't explicitly ask for the job.

When you have said the critical four words, **I WANT THIS JOB,** you have executed the fifth and final element of the basic sales techniques process, which is to ask for the order, known in the sales profession as "Close 'em".

When you say the critical four words **I WANT THIS JOB**, your pulse will be racing, you will be at your highest and best mentally. Now you must do something very important that will be very difficult to do. Just shut up. Yes, I really mean it, shut up! In the annals of sales lore, *usually whoever speaks first at this point loses the advantage, or loses the order.*

You have waited 8 seconds now, and your ride on the big bull at the rodeo seems like a long, long time, to quote country singer Vince Gill. Another 5 seconds goes by and you're really feeling the heat. That's OK. Everybody feels this way. The interviewer is also feeling this, probably to a lesser degree, but they are feeling it. If you get an objection from the interviewer at this point, answer it directly, close 'em again, and shut up again. If you have the courage to do this, you will win much of the time.

When you are experiencing the period of silence and you're feeling the pressure, it is comforting to know that this is the correct thing to do. There is nothing wrong with being silent at this point. No one will chastise you for it, and there is nothing rude about it. The interviewer isn't thinking about you in those few seconds. They are thinking about how they are going to respond. So just sit there and count slowly. That big bull isn't so hard to ride after all.

Closing means asking for the order – the job offer – as many times as feels appropriate. But what's appropriate? There is a point at which you run the risk of crossing the line between being assertive and being obnoxious from the interviewer's point of view, something you do not want to do. You won't increase your chances of getting the offer; in fact, you could lose the offer because you pissed them off.

So how do you recognize this line as you approach it and take steps not to cross it?

You look for negative clues from the interviewer just as you have looked for positive clues while trying to make the sale. Negative clues can be obvious as in outright statements of rejection, disbelief, or dislike about something in your background or something you just said.

More subtle clues are given all the time during the interview, especially when things are not going well. These include **negative body language,** such as the interviewer looking away a lot when they are talking to you; arms folded across their chest in a defensive posture; not speaking very much; lack of pleasantries: no smile; no laughter; no offers of *Can I get you something?*; signs of impatience (looking at their watch).

Positive body language includes smiles, laughing at a comment you make, leaning toward you rather than away, a pleasant, helpful tone of voice, allowing the interview to go on longer than you expected.

Body language, this unspoken communication, along with their spoken comments, will give you some insight as to what the interviewer really believes about you, either positive or negative. Sometimes just asking the interviewer outright can get an honest answer about if things don't seem to be going well in the interview. Sometimes closing again in a different manner will get their sincere attention again, or reinforce the positive aspects of the interview.

After you have asked for the job at least twice and you have *not* received a favorable response:

1) Ask if there is any other question that they would like to ask;

2) Ask if you have answered their questions to their satisfaction; and then

3) Close again by pulling out your **30-day Plan** for their company.

YOUR 30-DAY PLAN

The **30-Day Plan** is your idea in written format of what you imagined that you would do in your first 30 days on the job to start your job off with a bang. Keep it short, one page in length, using an outline format and bullet points. Make it something that the interviewer can read in 15 to 20 seconds.

Begin with a day of orientation, the usual stuff, and then use your imagination to describe what you would like to do. Propose an idea you have about the job in question (this is the most important part of the 30-day Plan).

Whatever your line of work is, take aspects of that and create activities around it. Explore the company's goals and expectations. Perhaps suggest something related to an article you just read about the company, an idea about cutting costs, a PR initiative, or an advertising notion. Keep it simple.

If you can get a question back from the interviewer, you just re-started the interview, even if it's for a minute or two. You will probably have improved the chemistry between the two of you and certainly your interview will be memorable to the interviewer.

Whatever you have in your plan may be similar to what they have in mind, or at the other extreme be creative but impractical to do. It doesn't really matter. What matters is that you will have done something dramatic that sets you apart from the competition.

TIP: By researching and drawing up your 30-day Plan you will show them that you put in extra effort to learn who they are and what their business is, and how important this job is to you.

Believe me, you will have grabbed their attention. You will impress them as being a cut above and they will remember you for it. Hardly any seasoned candidates do this, let alone inexperienced candidates.

Case in Point:

How effective is this 30-day Plan idea? A colleague and personal friend of mine, Professor Bob G., recently called me for advice concerning a friend of his in the law profession. His friend was trying to find a better place to work in Oakland, California and had become a finalist for a job he wanted. But things had bogged down and the firm couldn't make up its mind because the candidates involved were very strong and perhaps equally qualified. I explained my 30-day Plan idea to Bob, who then explained it to his friend. The friend submitted a plan to the client and he got the job. The 30-day Plan broke the logjam.

Now you are familiar with the basic selling process and how it relates to the job interview.

Here's a recap of the techniques to follow in the interview that you may use in creating your personal interviewing action plan:

- Start the interview at the first opportunity with a benefit statement

- Ask open-ended questions to get the interviewer to reveal what is important to them

- Use proof sources when you make an important statement about yourself and your experience

- Overcome objections or concerns raised by the interviewer by answering the easy objection directly, and the hard ones with a summary of benefits you previously stated

- Ask for the job!

THE INITIAL INTERVIEW WITH MANAGEMENT

If they like you after the initial interview with management, they (probably the hiring manager) will ask you to meet other people you would work with if you get hired. This second interview could be a few days down the road after they have interviewed all of their first-cut candidates, or it could be immediate. It's not unusual, especially in small companies, for an interviewer to say at the end of the interview, *Do you have a few minutes right now? I want you to meet someone else on the "team."* This is a very powerful buying signal on their part.

Don't be lulled into thinking you have the job in the bag, though. These impromptu meetings after the main interview are not informal, courtesy *Let's just shoot the bull a little* conversations. They can and do determine who gets to be a finalist. If one or two of the team members has something important to say about you later and it is negative, you are probably history as far as this company is concerned. The opposite is also true. If you really connect with someone and impress them, even if the meeting lasts only 10 minutes, it's a big plus for you.

Case in Point:

After I had had about 6 years of selling experience in the high-tech business selling software, I had a successful interview in San Francisco with Drew H., the national sales manager of a company based near Boston. It was a small firm, under 100 employees, and the interview went very well. Two days later, I was invited to company headquarters for an interview with the "team" on very short notice, so I had to take a redeye into Logan Airport and arrived at about 6:30 am. The hotel was forty-five minutes away in the town of Waltham, near company headquarters. My first interview was at 9 am, so I had just enough time to change into business attire and show up with some energy on my face.

After a very cordial welcome by Drew, I began a series of interviews with two sales reps and the head of Admin., and was then guided down the hall to see some of the technical people.

> The first person I met was a very polite man in shirtsleeves, named David. We got on very well, and talked for about half an hour on sales-related technical matters and surprisingly (as I thought at the time), about personal likes and dislikes. All this was very friendly, informal conversation. Do you see where I'm going here?
>
> David was the president of the company.
>
> I learned this from Drew at lunch, and I hadn't had an inkling. Fortunately for me the interview with David had gone very well. We had established a good chemistry in our very short time together, and I got the job offer at dinner that night.

Treat **ALL** interviews as if you are speaking to the president of the company. You just might be.

I also want to mention something about so-called "small talk," the kind David and I engaged in. There's nothing small about it. The interviewer wants to see how you behave and what you think when things are "off the record." Stay *on the record* the second you walk in the door.

It should be clear to you by now that interviewing is not just about the work. Most of the "first-cut" candidates can do the work. When it gets down to the two or three "final-cut" candidates, factors *other than* the ability to do the work itself may decide it.

COMPANY CULTURE

One of the most important factors is company culture, and how and *if* they see you fitting in. If they don't, you probably won't get an offer. A singular exception is the type of candidate who is highly qualified for some difficult-to-fill position, an expert of some kind. In this case the company will swallow hard, hire the candidate, and put them in a gilded cage somewhere out of the mainstream where they won't be a negative influence on the culture.

Company culture is the collective personality of the company. It's a mosaic of past history, the influence of key company executives on business execution, the sense of togetherness (or not) of employees, the accessibility of management, the general atmosphere experienced in the workplace on a day-to-day basis, the moral foundation of the company mission, and the ethics of fulfilling the company mission in the way it does business daily.

It's related to the type of energy and feeling you get after spending even a short time there. Some places are electric and fun, or at least pleasant to be in. Others give you a feeling of gloom or stress. In many places you won't get much of a feeling at all, neither energy nor unpleasantness, a kind of a *show up 5 days a week/do your job/go home* kind of place. It's just a business and it's boring, but it provides a decent living. Whatever type of culture it is, it usually filters down from top management.

Both you, as the candidate, and the company have to make a decision as to whether you fit into the culture. It's difficult for you to determine this in advance unless you have a friend, associate or other contact in the company who is willing to talk frankly about it. Read between the lines when you ask about the culture. Some people will tell you they are happy there when they're really not. Look for the unspoken language we discussed earlier.

TIP: Do research in advance in trade journals, company blogs, books written about the company, any source that will give you insight as to what it's like to work there. What's the employee turnover like? What's the primary reason employees leave? Are there communal areas and do you see employees mingling with each other? Is the atmosphere one you would feel comfortable in? Any information you gather from present or past employees or from books and media sources will be very helpful to you during the interview and immediately after, when you must decide whether you want to pursue this opportunity further.

CHEMISTRY

Considerations besides your qualifications and appropriateness for the company culture are going on during the interview. The interviewer will also be looking for signs or feelings of positive energy from you, an aura of genuine friendliness, courtesy, creative curiosity, good body language, a pleasant professional appearance, a general feeling of likeability.

At the same time the interviewer may be thinking: *Can I control this person? Will they follow my direction? Are they going to be more trouble than they are worth; will they turn out to be a "project"?* In the trade, a "project" is a person that is hard to deal with; it could be that they just don't do what they are told to do in a timely manner, or they could be a whiner or a "downer" personality that has a negative effect on morale.

All of these dynamics point to **chemistry**. Chemistry is an emotional bond, a feeling of understanding between two or more people. It's as hard to get a handle on as company culture, and yet is as important in determining who moves forward in the interview process and who gets an offer. At the end of the day, after all candidates for the position have been interviewed and the interviewer sits back quietly to review everything, it's the "gut check" that decides it. Most good interviewers that I know have reflective capabilities and trust their gut instincts.

Chemistry is a huge factor in deciding who gets the job. All final candidates can probably do the work based on objective data, so a good interviewer will go beyond the empirical stuff and see how they "feel" about you.

The magic of chemistry is generally out of our conscious control. Fortunately, some interviewers will like you right away and it will be obvious in the way they treat you. Still, mostly because of different personality types, sometimes you will find that it impossible to establish good chemistry with the interviewer. The best way to encourage positive chemistry in the interview is to be your genuine self — no faking or acting. A good interviewer will see right through the act, and it will create mistrust. You're smart and well prepared so you know what to do. Just be your best self.

CHAPTER 5

THE BASIC FOUR QUESTIONS

"Strive not to be a success, but rather to be of value."
(Albert Einstein)

During the interview you will be asked a lot of questions and you might think that you will never know what these will be in advance. True for some, but not all.

Here's where you gain another advantage over your competition. Each of the **Basic Four Questions** covered in this chapter is **ALWAYS** asked in some form during every interview other than a screening. You must be prepared to answer each one thoroughly, creatively, and in a way that presents strengths about you as benefits for the interviewer.

1. **Who are you?**

2. **Why are you here?**

3. **What can you do for me?**

4. **Why should I hire you?**

The actual wording of the Four Questions may differ according to the interviewer's style, but the *substance* is always the same.

Who are you? (Your 2-Minute Bio)

Question one is usually simple and straightforward. You may have heard this phrased as "Tell me about yourself." This is the time to give **your 2-Minute**

bio. Keep it concise and cohesive, with facts about yourself that are *pertinent to this job*. You may want to include:

- A quick review of your last four years in college

- Why you studied what you did

- What became your passion

- Why you chose the career field you did

- What is important to you right now

- What you value in life (very appropriate to mention family, friends, where you live)

- Significant achievements so far (awards, certifications, and the like)

- What you want to achieve in your career and why

- What your view of your future is

While you will want to present a well-rounded picture of yourself, hobbies and personal interests usually aren't relevant (unless, again, they pertain specifically to this job). Generalities such as "I am a highly motivated, energetic, persistent, ambitious, likeable, persuasive, successful, and otherwise wonderful person, etc.," are not appropriate, either ... yet. Without context to what the interviewer/company is looking for, they have no real clout and will come across as clichés at this early point in the interview. Wait until you can link these attributes as benefits to the interviewer. The interviewer will decide for themselves over the course of the interview if the general strengths you claim relate to them.

Practice your final bio ahead of time and keep it reasonably close to the two-minute mark. If you go on and on without a clear end in sight, the interviewer will probably cut you off. On the other hand, if they like what they hear, they will ask you questions about specific points. That's a sign that they have started taking an interest in you. If and when that occurs, you're off the two-minute clock.

Why are you here?

What this question really means is, *Why are you interviewing at this particular time, for this particular job, and specifically, at my company?*

This is a good time to describe your "dream job," at least as you conceive it to be right now, and relate it specifically to this company. If you are right out of school and have little work experience, you must point to some example of leadership or any position of responsibility in school, an internship, or community service that you have performed in the recent past that produced positive, measurable results.

Anything that shows that you held a responsible position and/or produced results is important. Explain that you could produce similar results in the specific job you're interviewing for — in other words, benefits the company would gain by hiring you.

You might say: *Mr. G., the position we're talking about today requires the leadership skills similar to those that I learned during my internship with ABC Company last summer. I can now bring those skills and results to this position.*

Or, *As you can see by the artwork in my information packet that I produced during my advanced graphics class, I created the kind of quality work that this position demands.* Be ready to back up your claims with a specific example.

If times are tough and you've been out of work for a while and are looking for a decent, basic job in your field, tell the interviewer the truth in positive terms and as benefits to them. Say something like, *Yes, I have been unemployed in my field for six months, and that's why I was excited to hear about your opening here. Based upon my past experience of producing results in similar work, I'm sure that I can bring the same results to you. Here are some examples of my work, and I have quality references to back all of this up.* Again: be positive; link your prior experience and positive results to what the interviewer is looking for.

> *TIP: Never tell anyone that you are desperate for a job and will do anything. You'll eliminate yourself instantly. Desperation usually has a negative effect on people and makes you appear less desirable. Everything you do in the interview must be positive in nature. You'll see why this is important in Chapter 7.*

What can you do for me?

This question is both professional and personal in nature, and by personal I mean personal to the interviewer.

On the professional side the interviewer will probe to see what your standing is in your chosen field as it pertains to this job. Have you demonstrated in the past that you are good at your work? What successes have you had in any position? Did you stand out at something; did you produce results that they can verify? What can you do to help make the company succeed?

If you're experienced, give specific examples of past work that produced results or made you stand out. Show any leadership positions you held in organizations related to your profession, any presentations you made to these groups. Frankly, just being a member of such a professional group can be important. Give examples of any extra things you did for previous employers or supervisors that went above and beyond what was expected. For example, maybe you initiated a plan to help your department and another part of the organization coordinate efforts that improved efficiency.

If you're just out of school, describe what leadership or responsible positions you held in campus organizations. Just to get you thinking:

- Were you a member of the Accounting Forum, the Associated Students, the Marketing Club, a social or community service organization?

- Were you a *leader* in such an organization?

- Did you join the ROTC?

- Did you work your way through school? (This will really impress them.)

- Did you study abroad during the summer?

- What kind of internships did you have? What were your responsibilities there? Did you produce any results?

- Were you a teaching assistant to a professor in your major?

- Did you volunteer for the food drive or something similar, on campus or in the community?

- Any of these experiences, described with specific results achieved, can impress an interviewer. They will help answer the professional side of the question, "What can you do for me?"

TIP: If you are in your second or third year on campus, get involved in organizations or clubs around your major to expand your knowledge of the field. Also start thinking about getting involved in something above and beyond your studies to broaden your experience, skills and maturity in preparation for the job interviews to come.

The Hidden Interview

Now, on the personal side, the interviewer will probe to see how you will have an effect on them personally if you got the job. They wouldn't be very smart if they didn't. The interviewer is looking for information that points to what you can do to make *them* succeed. They engage in what I call the **hidden interview**.

Based upon how you look, how you behave in the interview, how you respond to their questions, and how strong your experience is, the interviewer will ask themselves some very personal questions: *Will hiring you make my job easier to do? Can you hit the ground running? Can I trust you? Are you a reliable person who won't get me into trouble with my boss or my boss's boss? Will hiring you make me look good to my boss? Will you help me succeed, meaning, will I get promoted and make more money? Can I go to my boss with enthusiasm and say, "I found a great candidate for that job opening I have, and s/he looks like a real winner?"*

These are questions that the interviewer would never ask outright of you, but you should be aware that their evaluation of your value to them personally is going on beneath the surface of all standard interviews. Knowing this in advance, you can formulate some of your answers based upon your knowledge of what is going on in the interviewer's mind.

Yes, there is always something personal in it for the interviewer /hiring manager. When you consider that approximately 20% of all new hires don't make it past the first year for whatever reason, you can see why things can get real personal for the hiring manager — your success or failure will reflect directly on them.

Why should I hire you?

This is where you must concentrate on translating your strengths into benefits to the company that specifically relate to helping them make, raise, and/or save money. There are probably at least two or three other candidates that are as qualified as you. Tell them why it should be *you*.

If your interview has lasted at least forty minutes (and hopefully fifty minutes to an hour), it's a good sign that the interviewer is interested in you. They wouldn't have spent that much time and energy on you if you hadn't shown them something that impresses them. Now is the time to summarize all the benefits that were agreed to in the interview so far, and close 'em.

Remember, bottom line, the interviewer is looking for the following (covered in detail in Chapter 3):

1. Have you shown a history of successfully moving something from point 'A' to point 'B', i.e., have you gotten measurable or at least recognizable results in whatever it is that you have been doing?

2. Have you demonstrated that you have significant knowledge or expertise, or both, in doing the things related to this job?

3. Are you passionate about at least some aspect of your work?

4. If the interviewer feels that you have at least two out of these three attributes, you will probably move on to the next stage of the interviewing process, or even get an offer at this point.

Now that you have explained to them why you would be an asset to their company, you must close for the job again. Use the following language or something *very* close: *Mr./Ms. Smith, have I answered all your questions to your satisfaction? Yes. After hearing what you have said about your company and the specifics of the job, I am convinced that I want to come to work for you.* ***I want this job!***

The first few times you state this during your many-years-to-come of inter-viewing, it will take a little courage to do it. Fine. Just do it. Interviewers expect all serious candidates to do it, and if you don't, you definitely hurt your chances.

This step is so important that I'm going to give you a personal example of what happens when you don't do it:

Case in Point:

After I had a few years of successful sales experience, I went to an inter-view in downtown San Francisco. The company was a small but very successful software company headquartered in Atlanta and the inter-viewer was a very friendly fellow with a strong Southern accent that put me at ease immediately. I listened carefully and cited examples from my background that he agreed would be beneficial to his company. We established a very good chemistry and actually joked and laughed dur-ing the 50 minutes or so I was there.

I answered all of his questions truthfully and to his satisfaction. The interview was moving along about as well as I could have hoped for, and we were on a first name basis by now, so at the appropriate time I asked, "Roy, are there any other questions that you have for me?" He said No, and asked if I had any more for him. *No*. Silence ensued. After just a few seconds, he shook his head and said, "Ken, I just wish that you had asked for the job."

I felt my stomach drop, and the smile on my face vanished. Why I didn't ask for the job is still somewhat of a mystery to me, because *I did want the job*. I knew better, and I blew it. Perhaps I let my guard down because it was a very friendly interview. I'll never know the full story ... except that I didn't get the job and I still remember the humiliation I felt in the presence of this good man.

If you decide during the interview that you want the job, **close 'em**. *Always* ask for the job in a declarative way, in clear, specific terms. I highly recom-mend: **"Ms./Mr. Smith, I want this job."**

OTHER QUESTIONS YOU MIGHT BE ASKED

The Basic Four Questions provide a framework from which the interviewer formulates other questions. Most other questions of a general nature will be a subset of the Four.

In preparing for the interview, most of your time should be spent on the core issues of the specific position you're vying for, since *all* questions in the interview emanate ultimately from one unspoken request from the interviewer, "Convince me that you can do this job."

Be professional at all times, especially when and how you answer questions. You want to be real, natural, your true self. Be yourself but don't let your guard down completely. Think about what you're going to say before you open your mouth — once it's out, it's out. The interviewer is not your *pal* or *friend*, regardless of how much the two of you hit it off. It ain't Facebook. Interviewers will use the information that you give to evaluate you in *their* terms. Some information, if given carelessly or thoughtlessly, *will* be used against you.

With those caveats in mind, here is a short list of **general questions** that you should review and be prepared for in very broad terms, i.e., to tap into your personal, collegiate and work experiences and help you produce an impressive answer on the spot.

This list is not meant to be exhaustive in any way. And again: *Do not* memorize these 20 questions or any answers to them or you risk coming across canned or worse, tongue-tied because you can't remember your memorized answer. Just get familiar with them so that you can more easily think on your feet when it counts.

1.) Tell me something that you are passionate about.

2.) Name the greatest success that you have achieved in your life so far.

3.) Why did you choose (accounting, finance, marketing, basket weaving, etc.) as your chosen career field?

4.) Give me an example of a serious mistake you made in the past, and what you did about it, or learned from it. "I can't think of any," as former President George W. Bush stated in a town hall meeting when running for re-election in 2004, is not an option for you.

5.) Have you learned more from your successes or from your failures? Why?

6.) Why do you think that you are effective in dealing with people? (Give a specific example here of how you got someone or a group to follow your lead which produced favorable results. This shows that you were an effective manager.)

7.) Give me an example of an ethical dilemma you faced in your past and how you dealt with it.

8.) Give me an example of something you undertook above and beyond your normal job/school responsibilities. Why did you choose to do this? What was the outcome?

9.) What was the most challenging thing you undertook as a student/ employee, and how did you deal with it?

10.) Do you think that the customer is always right? Why? Why not?

11.) What do you expect from your boss? (A good answer here might be about having them trust and support you.)

12.) Describe your dream job (if you haven't already done so).

13.) How do you handle failure? (This is similar – but not exactly the same – to question 4 above.)

14.) Describe an action you took that was criticized by other employees/ students, and how you handled it.

15.) What was the most useful criticism you ever received?

16.) In a nutshell, what is your philosophy of management (or: working with others; selling; ethical behavior; anything that relates to the basics of the job)?

17.) What do you consider to be the greatest achievement in your professional life so far?

18.) Why do you want to leave your current job?

19.) Give me a good reason why I shouldn't hire you? (This is the type of question designed to try to trip you up, or to create stress. A good answer: "Mr. X, I didn't come here not to be hired.")

20.) Have you ever been fired?

MEMORIZING QUESTIONS

DON'T.

There are hundreds of potential questions that could be asked by the interviewer in any interview because the interviewers keep changing for the candidate and the candidates each have a different background in education and experience.

Students and job candidates have routinely asked me for examples of questions that might be asked, but I can only take them so far. Beyond the Basic Four, you will never know what specific questions you will be asked in the interview. Never.

Because this point is so important for you the candidate, I will state again: *Memorizing long lists of potential questions along with canned answers to them is largely futile and actually dangerous.* You could get confused as to which answer goes with what question when you are under pressure. If this happens, you have really hurt your chances for a successful interview.

TIP: Even if you asked one of your professors what questions you might expect on their final exam, this just isn't done in the big leagues. So step up to the plate and familiarize yourself with (not memorize) commonly asked questions in the interview (I have provided several in this book). Then, during the interview, you can come up with creative, convincing answers on the spot. When you do this you will really impress the interviewer, believe me. There is no substitute for being in the moment, being authentic, and thinking on your feet.

Bottom line: Be sure you take your best tool for answering questions with you to the interview. Your best tool is *you*. Just make sure it's sharp before you go in.

QUESTIONS TO ASK THE INTERVIEWER

You must not only be familiar with your target company's website, but also prepare six or seven questions for the interviewer. They will expect this, and it will go against you if you don't have them prepared. I'm talking about **well-thought-out, cogent questions that relate *specifically* to the position in question**. Remember, it's all about how you explain your strengths in terms of benefits to the company. Listen carefully to the interviewer's answers and be prepared to provide an appropriate response. Even at this early stage of your career, point out specific examples in terms of results achieved in the past, and relate these to how you can help them now.

Now you know that the Basic Four Questions and general questions from the interviewer's perspective. At this point let's construct yours.

Here are some suggested **questions of a general nature** that you might want to ask the interviewer:

1. *What would you expect from me if I were to work for you in this job? How would my performance be measured?* (Listen carefully to their response and then give an example of how you achieved results in the past related to their answer, along with a proof source. A proof source here might be a former boss, professor, colleague, an award you received, a promotion you got. The example that you give here is a benefit statement related to something specific that they are looking for and is a powerful closing tool.)

2. *What kind of support can I expect to help me realize the goals that you would set for me?*

3. *Would you please describe the company culture for me as you see it?*

4. *You obviously like working for your company. Can you tell me why?* (If you like what you hear, state that these are the things that you are also looking for. This is a great way to build rapport with the interviewer toward the end of the interview.)

5. *What in your opinion makes new hires that work for you successful in their jobs?* (Take what the interviewer says here and explain why

you have the same characteristics as those of their successful employees and relate these to successes you have had in the past.)

6. *What's a typical day like for those that work for you?* (After they describe it, express how it confirms why you want to work there.)

7. *What would you say is the main reason that some of your new hires fail?* (Now's your chance to explain why this won't happen to you.)

8. *What's the most important thing a new hire working for you can do to be successful?* (If you have an experience from the past that relates to what the interviewer states, now is the time to bring it up.)

9. *What are the things that you most admire in an employee?* (If any of these things relate to you, point them out.)

10. *Your assistant is very attractive, can I get their number?* (On second thought, better to ask this after you get the job – or not at all!)

11. *If you were to hire me, what's the most important thing I could do for you in the first 90 days on the job?* (If you think you can do it, say so. This is an excellent way of boosting the interviewer's confidence in you as a candidate.)

12. *Do you have recognition programs for employees who over-achieve?* (If you like what you hear, say something to the effect that a healthy competitive environment is the place where you do your best and that it motivates you to do more than what's expected of you. Ask this question *only if you mean it*. The interviewer will remember you for it, I promise.)

13. *Is there a fast-track to promotion for employees who do well in your company?* (This question shows that you're not just an average candidate and expect to produce positive results right away. But take care it doesn't come off sounding cocky.)

14. *Do you have training programs that would help me produce my best results as soon as possible? Could you please briefly describe your basic training program?* (This question shows the interviewer that you are raring to go, if you are hired.)

15. *Are there any new products/initiatives/projects on the horizon in your company that you can talk about in brief today?* (This ques-

tion shows that you are excited about going to work for them, that you are ambitious, assertive, and really want to get "down home" with the interviewer. If they mention something that excites you, say so. They will like you for it. However, don't ask this question if you just want a regular 8 to 5 job and want to do your best but nothing extra. Also, don't ask it if your research shows that the company isn't noted for forward thinking or new initiatives. They may just want to do a very good job day-to-day.)

16. *If you hire me, and in the course of doing my job I suggest an idea that would help me do my job better and get better results, would you consider it?* (If they say yes, which they should do, it shows that they are probably an open company, that is, open to new ideas. This is a positive sign for you. If they say "It depends," they are either cautious around interviewees, or perhaps they're a bit stodgy and you will have to decide how important that is to you. Most effective companies are open to considering new ideas. Again, asking this question shows the interviewer that you are a cut above the ordinary candidate.)

17. *This has been an excellent interview from my perspective, and I would like to ask you at this point: Do you think that I can do this job? I do.* (Obviously, ask this question only if you are sure you want this job, or at least want to advance to the next round. This is also a professional, assertive way to ask for the job, which you must do at this point, anyway.)

Add your own questions, in your own style.

THE NEXT STEP

Never leave the interview without getting agreement on a "next step" — this means a statement from them that they want to see or hear from you again – tomorrow, next week, whenever.

You can go down one of two paths.

The first path is the one in which the interviewer gives you a next step without your having to ask for one. This is very positive, of course; it means that you have established yourself as a serious candidate, maybe a finalist, for the position.

Next steps include scheduling your next meeting with someone else in the company, an invitation to visit company headquarters, a specific time for you to call them back, a referral to another colleague of theirs (who may be just down the hall), another interview with the same person, or a request for your references. If the interviewer asks, "When could you start?", *you got the job*, barring any unforeseen problems with references, social websites, or any other source of information that might put you in a bad light later on.

The second path is more difficult: *You* must ask for the next step yourself. If the interviewer says, "We'll get back to you" or "Someone from HR will get back to you," that is not a next step. You must try to get some kind of agreement that you can contact them in the very near future by whatever medium. *Ms. Allen, will it be all right if I call you/e-mail you tomorrow after you have interviewed all of your candidates? No? Would next Tuesday or Wednesday be OK?* You need to show that you want this job and are attaching some urgency to finding out what they have decided.

If they won't give you a next step or are vague about it, you're in trouble. State politely that you sense some reluctance on their part. *Was there anything that I didn't explain completely, or to your satisfaction? Can I clarify anything?* State again that you are positive that you can do this job well, if you really feel it. This may be just what they are waiting to hear.

They may tell you that it is company policy for them to contact the candidate, not the other way around. At that point, tell them that you understand and stand up to leave, and as you do, hand them a copy of your **30-day Plan**, if you have not already done so, and explain briefly what it is. This is the type of dramatic move that I mentioned earlier. Since it's almost never done by anyone, you might just stop them in their tracks, maybe restart the interview, and even get a next step. And if you have had the time to create your personal information packet, drop it on them.

Now you've done the best you can. Smile, thank them again, and leave.

If you decide during the interview that you don't want the job, thank them sincerely for their time and effort on your behalf, and leave in a gracious manner. You will now probably be put in their HR candidate bank and you could meet again in the future under different circumstances if you stay in their industry, and especially if their business expands.

It's also not unheard of to have the interviewer refer you on to another manager in their company if you really impressed them. You may not be what they are looking for right now, but maybe someone else in the company has an opening of interest.

I have collected fees for candidates who got jobs from referrals of just this kind. In fact the largest fee I ever collected was for Doug G., an experienced candidate of mine who was interviewing for a sales manager position at a very successful and growing technical company in Silicon Valley. He so impressed the first interviewer that he was immediately introduced to the VP of Sales. Two interviews later he became the Director of Sales for the entire company. So Doug not only got a job but also a *promotion* at the same time.

TIP: Even if you decide against taking the job and everything else in the interview went very well, send them a short, personal thank you note. This will help them remember you for future possibilities, and you just made the interviewer a member of your personal network.

THE HIRING FILTER AND HIRING PROCESS CHECKLIST

As further assistance to you during the early years of your adventures in interviewing, I have included in Appendix A some additional insights as to what the interviewer is thinking during the interview. One of the best and most lucrative of my clients provided its management team with what they called a **Hiring Filter** — a simple cheat sheet to assist their new and young management team in interviewing candidates. The company was expanding rapidly and there was no time to train managers, especially young new managers, in interviewing techniques. Many of them had never interviewed any candidate prior to being hired themselves. Sound like anyone we know?

Also included from the same client is a **Hiring Process Checklist**, which encapsulates the recruiting process as a whole. This is somewhat similar to the one used by airline pilots, although much simpler. When you're working 10-12 hour days, including some Saturdays, as this company's managers were, it's easy to forget even basic HR procedures.

TIP: *What's valuable for the interviewer to know is doubly valuable for you. Make sure to review the* **Hiring Filter and Hiring Process Checklist** *in Appendix A.*

CHAPTER 6
POST INTERVIEW

*"In order to get from what **was** to what **will be**, you must go through **what is**."* (Anonymous)

SENDING NOTES AND OTHER FOLLOW UP

Whether it is the first or even the fourth interview, be sure to send a personal note to the interviewer the very same day. Send an e-mail too; the e-mail insures that you get in touch again right away just in case the interviewer gets called out of town suddenly. Snail mail will be the other reinforcing message a day or two later. Texting, tweeting and/or other social media formats are unacceptable for a follow-up note unless the company you're interviewing with is a social media entrepreneur. (Screening interviews do not warrant a follow-up note.)

Most interviewers expect a personal handwritten note from people that they consider to be a serious candidate. It's simple protocol, and it sets you apart from those who don't do it. Remember, we're working on as many positive things as we can to help you stand out from the competition. Even small gestures are important, and they do add up.

If you have decided that you don't want the job you interviewed for but think there is a possibility that you might work for this firm in the future, send a personal note. You just might get a favorable note from the interviewer filed in the company database for a call the next time an appropriate position opens up.

In addition, a handwritten note shows them that you feel they are important enough to you that you took the time and made the effort. However, if you don't write well in cursive, as so many of today's college graduates do not, make sure that someone has read your note in advance to be sure it is legible. Don't be like the doctor who scribbled out a prescription for a patient that's illegible and the patient got the wrong prescription. If your handwriting can't be easily read, type it, but *handwrite* your signature.

Keep it short. Interviewers/hiring managers have lots of things to read in their busy day, and a long note from you just might be tossed onto a pile of "things to do later." Short (less than 100 words) means that they will read it now.

What to include? Mention one or two of the highlights of the interview, and thank the interviewer for their time and effort again. Express your true feelings of excitement about their opportunity.

> *TIP: Add something "new" to say: Mention an article about the company in the media that did not come up for discussion in the interview, for instance, or an article about the particular discipline connected with the position. Relate the article to one of the benefits you will bring to the company that you mentioned in the interview. This adds interest to the note and will help them remember you as the professional you are.*

Finally, if you don't have one, ask for the next step again, even if it is just to state, "I look forward to hearing again from you soon." They just might contact you and say, "I'll call you by the end of the week, and thanks for your note. That article you mentioned in it was very interesting."

If the interviewer asked you not to call, *don't*. Respect their wishes. When pushing for a job you really want, there's a fine line between being professionally proactive and being too aggressive. If you are looking for an outside sales job, being a little over-aggressive is OK. In most other jobs it's not.

ORAL AND WRITTEN OFFERS

If you got an oral job offer on the spot, Congratulations!

TIP: It's perfectly OK to accept on the spot: you can get some good upfront benefit from this by showing that you're enthusiastic and really want the job.

Let's say that you have just gone through your final interview, had a discussion of job responsibilities, salary and start date, and shook hands on it. The interviewer/decision-maker will say something like "Welcome aboard," if you accept on the spot. They will then tell you that they will prepare an **offer letter** (which outlines the details of your employment) for your review and signature, or in other cases tell you that you will be signing an **employment contract** at HR. Either way, legally you do not have a job until you sign the employment document *and return it to them.*

Something to be aware of, however: oral offers or promises are legal but may not be enforceable, especially if there are no other witnesses to the offer. Yes, 99% of oral promises are consummated with an offer letter or contract, but occasionally promises unravel. For instance, you may be dealing with someone who, shortly after promising you the position, finds someone they like a lot better and calls you to say the deal is off. Again, it's rare, but it does happen, and you have no real recourse (what are you going to do, sue them?).

If you are told to expect an offer letter, you should ask if you could wait for the letter or pick it up later the same day so that you can review it right away.

When you get the offer letter in the mail or via e-mail, or when you get to review it with a company representative in person, you should ask for twenty-four hours to think it over and review the offer with your spouse, significant other, trusted friend, mentor, or parent, especially if one of these is a professional in your field of endeavor, company executive, etc. Most companies won't have a problem with this. They understand how important all of this is to you.

Besides, there will be things in the letter that you have to review. You will have already discussed job responsibilities, whom you will report to, and specifics of the job description. Now you should look carefully at official job title, salary and other compensation, employee benefits (especially health), performance review dates, and yes, severance and termination specifics.

These twenty-four hours will also give you time to evaluate any other "irons in the fire" that you had going. Maybe you were very close to getting an offer for another position that you liked as much, or better. This calls for serious analysis on your part *right now*. Contact the second company to find out where they are in the decision-making process as far as your application is concerned and tell them outright what your position is. If you actually are a finalist with them, they will level with you. Get an understanding in a respectful way that it has to be *today*. It may be that they can't make a decision about you today because of where they are in the interviewing process. Oh well, you tried, and now is the time to make your choice.

If you don't get back to the decision-maker at the other company who gave you an offer letter in the agreed-upon time, they will begin to have doubts about you. *But twenty-four hours, or just over the weekend if your interview was on a Friday, is all you get.* After all, they have made an important decision for their company and want an answer in a timely manner. If you push it to forty-eight hours or more, they will probably think that you are playing them off on another opportunity, and they won't like it. This is no way to start off in a new job. Everything now should be about how excited you are about getting this position and joining their company, if you really want to.

> *TIP: Perhaps the most important thing you can do post-interview in evaluating whether this is the job for you, is to do your own "gut check." This is the time for being true to yourself and thinking about what makes you happy. Whatever it is — money, a promotion in your career field, the geographic location of the company, a chance to work with leaders in your field, or, perhaps, an opportunity to increase your professional knowledge — **heed it**. If you choose against your self-knowledge and/or gut instincts, it won't be long before you start to experience miserable Monday mornings.*

MONEY – WHEN TO TALK ABOUT IT... WHEN NOT TO... and THE IMPORTANCE OF NEGOTIATION

Never bring up the subject of money, (i.e., salary, commission, bonuses) until a job offer has been made. If the interviewer brings up the subject before an offer has been made, deal with it right away, but *you* should not bring it up for discussion until they offer you a job because it will be considered presumptuous and inappropriate on your part. It's also completely irrelevant if they wind up not making you an offer.

You should have a good idea of what to expect in the way of compensation before you leave for the interview. There are plenty of sources and job search sites mentioned in Appendix C, where you can check out the current marketplace for compensation. It's best to go in with a range in mind so when a job offer has been made and they ask you what kind of compensation you are looking for, you can politely and confidently state your range.

Being prepared in advance for this discussion, you will understand why you do yourself a disservice if your range is too low, and how you can eliminate yourself from consideration if your range is too high. Simply put, if your compensation range is too low, you will not be paid what you are due and it will take you years to catch up, if you ever do. If your range is too high (that is, higher than their established company range for your position), you could eliminate yourself from contention. In larger companies it takes a senior-level person to make an exception to salary policy.

If the interviewer gives you a compensation package after an offer has been made without asking you what you want, ask for time to consider it, as mentioned above.

Female candidates should be especially prepared with a compensation range to protect your interests, both short and long-term (see the suggested list of online resources in Appendix C). It would disconcert you (at the very least!) to know how many companies still offer a female candidate a lower starting compensation base than a male candidate for the same position, and that some female candidates are unaware of this practice.

Not only is it illegal but it could mean tens of thousands of dollars lost to you as an employee at this company over the years because future salary raises and bonuses are determined by current salary. For example, if a female candidate starts out at 15% below her male counterpart for the same position it will add up to a bunch over the course of your time with that company. You do the math. But, you say, that you'll be changing jobs 8 to 12 times during your career and will make up the difference in compensation along the way. Maybe not.

> *TIP: Many companies will base their starting compensation offer when you change jobs on what you are currently being paid. All candidates should review compensation ranges for the type of job you're interviewing for before you interview.*

GIVING NOTICE AT YOUR PRESENT JOB

If you've been working for another company, be sure to give your current employer adequate notice (two weeks is the standard, but it is not usually a requirement; check your employment agreement/contract).

If your departure is a surprise to them, they will need more than two weeks to replace you, and this can cause hardship for them. Giving proper notice is the professional thing to do. If you dump them out of hand with no notice, you might pay for it later in your career; even in large industries, word gets around. Don't forget that the prospective employer will call "unofficial" references, such as employees they may know at your former company. If you get a reputation of walking away from companies without giving notice, it will work against you in the future.

IF YOU DONT GET AN OFFER (ALSO KNOWN AS REJECTION)

Even if you do everything well in the interview process and they appear to like you, you still may not get the job. Most of the time you will never find out why, that is, what the *real* reasons are. Companies are very tight-lipped about this type of information and many times won't even tell recruiters who represent you why you didn't get the job.

Typical follow-up answers you might get from a company spokesperson (like HR) or your recruiter or headhunter would be:

- *We had an excellent group of candidates for the position; you came in right near the top.*

- *You came in second.*

- *All they told me was that they liked someone else better.*

- *We felt that you didn't have enough experience, compared to the other candidates.*

- *We felt that you were over-qualified.*

- *We'll keep your resume on file for future reference.*

Most rejections, if you were a serious candidate, come in the appearance of a form letter drafted by an Admin. or HR person with phrases similar to the above. Whatever it is, it's crap; the company is trying to protect itself from potential lawsuits. In some cases you won't hear anything at all, and your calls will be referred to HR.

TIP: If you are on very good terms with the recruiter, if one is involved, or if you know someone personally in the company, you might get some meaningful answers about why you didn't get hired. It's worth following through on this because if you do get an honest, objective answer it will help you avoid the same mistakes (if you made any) in future interviews.

Of course, there are plenty of instances in which the candidate who gets the job is the one who knows someone in the company who is influential, not because they are the best qualified. Candidate selection can also be determined by company internal power struggles and other politics. Most of these are unfathomable and neither you nor your recruiter will ever know the nasty details.

Unfortunately, you lost this time out. Second place means almost nothing here, unless you really were a close second. In that case, a referral to another internal manager or a manager acquaintance in another company could happen if they were really impressed by you. But you can't count on it.

After getting very close to an offer, whether in fact or just in your own mind, you will feel the pain of rejection. It hurts no matter who you are. So, take a deep breath and move on. At the very least you have learned something valuable in this process for future use.

Remember your support group? Go there.

CHAPTER 7

ABOVE AND BEYOND THE INTERVIEW: THE CRUCIAL INTANGIBLES

"Integrity is the essence of everything successful."
(R. Buckminster Fuller)

The following sections provide a more thorough discussion of various subjects touched on in previous chapters.

CHEMISTRY REDUX — A PERSONAL PERSPECTIVE

People hire people after a face-to-face-meeting. There are very few exceptions to this, even for people hired overseas who may never meet their hiring manager in person again after the hiring interview. And after all interviews have been completed and all data are evaluated for a particular position, it's a gut check by the employer that decides it.

A very important element of the gut check is the chemistry that was created (or wasn't) during the interview. Chemistry not only goes a long way in influencing the decision-maker's choice of candidate but also is a good indicator of who will be successful in the job. Interviewers for high-paying sales positions know that the candidate who gets the job must perform in a highly competitive environment and that establishing good chemistry with customers can decide who gets the order or who doesn't.

Case in Point:

After three years of successful major account selling experience with Xerox in San Francisco, I was given responsibility for Bechtel Corporation, one of Xerox's most important accounts in the country. One of my responsibilities was selling supplies. After about a year on the account and having established a significant level of rapport and trust, Bechtel gave me an opportunity to bid on a very large purchase of paper, about a six-month supply. The bidding wars were fierce; I knew that our high quality paper product was almost certainly not the lowest in price, but I translated all the qualities of the product into benefits for Bechtel, handed in the bid, and went back to my office, holding my breath to await the results. Late in the afternoon I got the call — my bid had won. *It was the largest non-government supply order in the history of supply sales for Xerox in San Francisco up to that time. I had just sold nine boxcars of paper.* That's railroad boxcars, not truckloads.

It wasn't the quality of product and price alone that got the order. Other companies had great products and prices, too. It was chemistry. I had established excellent rapport and trust with my client and always dealt with them in an honest and highly professional manner. In the end, I think that the decision-makers at Bechtel looked for reasons to give me this sale as a sign of their trust and faith in me.

The Bechtel order was unusual and a big win for me. But over the years, more large orders were won or big problems solved thanks to the magic of chemistry I established with large accounts such as Transamerica Corporation, Foremost-McKesson (now McKesson Corporation), and Southern Pacific Railroad.

These career experiences relate back to my interviews that got me the job at Xerox in the first place. I established good chemistry with the decision makers during my interviews, and I suspect they knew I could do the same with their customers. So can you.

On the flip side, negative chemistry is equally as powerful and as difficult to understand. At various times, in interviews, at work, and in life in general, you will meet people who immediately give you a bad feeling about them.

As a headhunter, I have placed dozens of candidates as sales people in the high tech industry. When a candidate of mine failed in the interview process, I always sought feedback from the client to find out why. In most cases the reasons for the failure of the candidate, according to the client, were about "not connecting" in the interview.

These were candidates with proven sales skills and a history of getting results, but they didn't get the job. Often the client had difficulty in explaining why. They would just fall back on the safe answer, "I just couldn't see them fitting in here." Almost certainly the failure was due to a lack of good, or at least moderately good chemistry between the candidate and the interviewer.

> TIP: When you encounter a negative atmosphere during an interview, especially an important interview, the only real effective thing you can do, in my opinion, is to continue at your polished best, keep your guard up, follow your plan, and hope that the chemistry/atmosphere improves. Again, strive for a next step in the process in hopes that you can get a later interview with someone you can "click" with. Don't fall into the "It's not fair" trap. It's not.

After a bad encounter, regain your footing by having a discussion with someone from your support group, and move on to the next opportunity.

NOTE-TAKING

Be certain to take a note pad with you to each interview. You will have at least six or seven questions that you composed the night before, and having them written down and available in your Final Prep Checklist / Interviewing Action Plan will help insure that you won't forget to ask them (see Ch. 3). It's also important to take notes during and immediately following the interview.

A lot will be going on in your head during the interview so it's especially helpful to make brief notes on important points that the interviewer is making to help you stay on topic and "in the moment"; you want to be focused on what they're saying or asking right now, not just on what your next statement's going to be.

The extensive notes should come after the interview when you have time. It's important to do this if the interview was an especially important one for you, or if the interviewer made a point that you want to follow up on later, or if you made a mistake and want to analyze why you made it. This is especially important for gaffes or any kind of blunder you think that you might have made. Everyone makes them, but making the same mistake again in a future interview could prove to be painful. Even though you will be tired at the end of the day, take the time to review the important points of each interview, plusses and minuses.

This process will get easier over time, and as you gain experience you won't have to do it as much. If you make the excuse that you just don't have time to go through this exercise and review what might be a gold mine of information about how you interview, just ask yourself how much time you have to be unemployed.

REFERENCES

Guard your references carefully. Don't hand them out to casual inquiries and don't put them on your resume — you don't want to inconvenience and antagonize your references by broadcasting their names all over the Web, exposing them to unwanted calls. Provide your reference list only to serious prospects and only when asked, which can happen immediately before or after the job offer is made. If it happens before the job offer is made, it's a sign that they are very serious about you, a big buying signal.

It should be obvious that you must call your references first and ask them if it is OK to use them as a reference. It's extremely presumptuous not to, and reflects poorly on you if you didn't take the time to do this, no matter how well you know the reference. Getting a call from a prospective boss should *never* come as a surprise to them.

Don't assume anything as far as references go. Let them know specifically which companies you intend to interview with and for which particular position. Call them once to alert them to the fact that you are interviewing in general, and ask for permission to use them as a reference. Call them again once you are asked by an interviewer to actually submit references.

If you are still in school, you will need to have at least one academic reference (better two or three), hopefully two professional work references, and one or two personal references.

Academic references should be as high-ranking as possible. A department head, a chairperson, a dean or a senior professor who can say that they saw you in action in class presentations, clubs, or community involvement activities and will discuss why they think that you could bring something valuable to the table, are most desirable. Referencing an instructor whose class you simply attended won't cut it. Remember, instructors deal with hundreds if not thousands of students throughout their careers: what made YOU stand out in their class?

Professional work references are, by far, the most important. These include managers from any paying job you had, especially if you held a responsible position of any kind. Managers from unpaid internships are also appropriate.

A personal reference must be someone you have actively worked with in the community, or someone of a professional nature who can vouch for you as a responsible person. This could be a clergyperson, a lawyer, a doctor, a manager of a business (even if you didn't work for them), or someone notable who has had a long-term relationship with you and your family and can vouch for your accomplishments and character, with specific examples.

> *TIP: Most people don't realize that asking for someone to be a reference is also like asking for a job. You've told them you are looking for a job: Would they have a job opening for you to look at, or know of someone who does? If the reference knows you well enough, they might make a phone call or two on your behalf and connect you directly to the hiring manager for a job opening that you weren't aware of. Your network, as you now know, is the main source of quality job leads, and this is an example of the potential power of that network.*

It will be uplifting to hear, after you get your great job from the hiring manager, that their conversation with one of your references influenced them a great deal. Stand up straight with pride when you hear them say, "Your reference, Mr. _, said that we would be fortunate to get you."

So take full advantage of what your references can do for you. Don't subject your reference to surprise or embarrassment by not contacting them before a hiring manager does. Call them in advance and be sure they are thoroughly briefed on what you are about to do. Call them *again* after a successful interview to let them know that you submitted them as a reference and that they might get a call. If they are the good reference you believe them to be, they will do what they can to help you.

A word of caution: using a reference from a current employer is a very tricky thing to do. Unless you were laid off and have a promise from your soon-to-be former boss that they will act as a good reference, don't tell anyone that you are going to leave unless you trust them implicitly. If you do tell someone in management that you are interviewing, they will look at you differently from that point on. You will no longer be considered as a member of the team. It's a cold thing to face but it's a fact and it could cause you serious harm.

This could be a potentially lethal situation ...

Case in Point:

A candidate of mine, Stan F., who worked for a high tech company in Silicon Valley during the technology explosion of the late nineties, became a victim of providing too much information to his current employer about the possibility of his leaving the company. Stan was smart, personable, a hard worker with about three years experience in his profession but unfortunately, also a little arrogant. People were moving on or moving up rapidly because of the incredible expansion of the industry at that time. He called me to discuss job opportunities. We had a productive talk and then he told me that, in an effort to assure me that he was a serious candidate, he was going to inform his boss that he was "looking around." I advised him not to do that because it would change the way he would be viewed within the firm. He went ahead and did it, anyway. The afternoon of the same day that he informed his boss of his "looking around," company security came to his cubicle along with his boss. Stan was fired right there, instructed to pack up his personal belongings and escorted out the door.

At some point in your career you may have a situation in which you get a job offer from another firm, you give proper notice, and your current company tries to "buy you back" with a promotion and more money. This would happen if your leaving would cause serious hardship for the company in the short run until they could replace you. If the buyback occurs, things will look good on the surface for all involved and everyone will appear to be happy, but the fact is that you will never be viewed the same again by management. They will assume, as far as they are concerned, that you are an opportunist and will continue to look around.

It's perfectly OK to "look around" while you are gainfully employed. It's an accepted practice in the work world, and as long as you are doing your current job to the full extent of your abilities and fulfilling your current responsibilities, there's nothing ethically wrong about it. Just be sure that you give proper notice — two weeks is the usual — if you do decide to leave for a better opportunity.

ALWAYS BE POSITIVE ABOUT EVERYTHING YOU SAY

Never say anything negative about anything during the interview. The interview is a sales proposition. Negatives of any kind, especially if introduced by you, just detract from the sales process.

Under normal circumstances, the interviewer should also be trying to sell to you, if they feel that you are a serious candidate. You probably won't hear anything negative from them unless they decide against you as a candidate, unless they are trying to test you, or unless their company has received some bad press recently and they want to discuss the situation with you honestly.

If something negative or potentially negative does come up about your background, and sometimes it will, explain it to them in a positive way, for example, *Yes, it's been ___ months since graduation and I haven't landed a career job yet, but I have used the time to put my management skills to work by taking on an unpaid internship at XYZ company. (And/or) I volunteer for ABC non-profit.* Be sure that what you say is the complete truth, but we'll get to that under the following section on Ethics.

If you are in your first career job and they ask you why you want to leave it or why you were laid off, answer directly, truthfully and positively. Never say anything bad about a former company or boss, especially a boss. In the interview world, dissing a former boss is considered a real no-no. For one thing, it violates interview protocol. For another, it makes you look like a sniveler or complainer and it's considered unprofessional.

If asked outright about your former boss (let's assume it was someone you hated), say something like, *I learned a lot from Mr. X, and although we didn't see eye-to-eye on some matters, he helped me gain extensive knowledge in the industry and exposed me to some influential contacts in the business, which will be valuable to me in the future.*

Interviewer: "So why do you want to leave Company XYZ?"

You: *Well, when I was newly hired, I spent my first year* (six months, whatever) *working long days learning the business. I was enjoying my work but was beginning to see that the career path that was described for me when I first came on board was not going to materialize as expected. This was mainly due to ____. I have nothing but good to say about the company and my co-workers, but things have changed and I have to consider moving on.*

At times you will be seriously tested. The interviewer may drill into an area of your background that may appear deficient to them.

Interviewer: "I see here that you manage a team of seven people at your company, and you have been doing this for six months or so — not a very long time. What was the most difficult thing you had to do during that time?" What the interviewer is trying to do here is to see how you handled yourself during a difficult situation and how you will explain it now, even if the entire experience at the time was negative.

Again, you must find a truthful way to put a positive spin on it. Think back: What did you *learn* from the experience? What will you not repeat? Or: What skill could you apply in a different job?

You: *The most difficult thing I had to do during my first six months was to ____. I had never done anything like this in the past. I remembered my training from the company and sought management help. I made sure that all of my facts were correct* (etc.). *This was a very stressful process for me, but I'm sure I did the best I could. My boss was satisfied and supported my decision.*

The interviewer may also test you by trying to get you into an argument with a controversial question or statement. This could be a shrewd move on their part or the interviewer may just be inexperienced, incompetent or prejudiced. You won't know and in any case, don't let yourself be pulled into an argument. Even if you are logically, rationally, or morally correct and you win the argument (at least in your own mind), you will still lose as far as progressing in the interview process, since a negative atmosphere has been created either on purpose or accidentally.

If you "win" the argument and the original purpose was to test you, you just might get heated enough to piss off the interviewer. Their purpose for testing you is to see how you would respond to a customer making the same comment and to see how you will generally react under pressure. So, regardless of the reason behind the provocation you must create a positive response and not provoke them in return.

Let's look at an example:

Interviewer: "There has been a lot of coverage lately in the media about gays in the military. How do you feel about this?"

Gulp!

You: *Well, Mr. J., I've read about this situation myself and I think that it is a complex one, and has important ramifications for not only the military but also for the nation as a whole. I haven't formed an opinion yet, but I will after I have had more time to consider it.*

Most likely you will have to give the type of answer a politician would give, i.e., evasive, non-controversial, but safe. You acted well under pressure, showed that you can think on your feet and could/would act in a professional, non-controversial manner in front of a customer of the firm and not get pulled into a dangerous no-win argument. That's how you handle an objective interviewer who is just trying to test you for a legitimate reason.

For a prejudiced interviewer, it's the same. Suppose you get a statement thrown at you that goes something like this:

Interviewer: "Our experience is that certain minorities don't do very well in their job responsibilities. Things just don't seem to work out very well for them."

So, you just got thrown a curve ball — What do you do?

You: *Mr. Y, my experience in working with people so far leads me to believe that most people deserve the benefit of the doubt until they can be judged by the results they produce. I believe that if a person was hired after they passed all tests, had the background to meet the requirements of the job, were trained well, and were supported well by their boss, they will probably do well regardless of their background.*

Yes, you might say it's another verbal dance, but one that just might get you past another landmine. Again, always be positive. No red flags. Don't forget, your objective here is to get an offer letter or to advance to the next round.

ETHICS

When most students I know are asked about the topic of **ethics**, they are aware of what it's about in general, but when questioned deeper it's evident that they know relatively little about the core elements. Usually their only exposure to ethics at the university level is from a philosophy or perhaps a law course.

All companies will hold you responsible for ethical breaches. These days, once you're hired you most likely will be required to take a variety of online tutorials about company policy and procedures including ethical behavior on the job and then sign a document stating that you took the courses. Later, should you be caught up in some kind of company scandal, even by association, you can't say that you didn't understand the situation. From the time you sign the ethics document, the company is off the hook as far as you're concerned and you're on it. It's called CYA.

"What does ethics have to do with my getting a job?" you may ask. A *lot*, not only about getting the job you want but also keeping it. If you commit an ethical infraction on your resume or during the interview (usually, lying) and you are caught, your interview is over and you are finished with that company for good. The interviewer will make a note in the company database that states simply that you lied and any future attempt by you to get employment there, even years down the road, will be futile. This is true for literally all companies. *They will assume that if you lied about something during the interview process you will lie about something else and they want nothing to do with you.*

My discussion of ethics is going to be a practical one related to your getting and keeping a great job. I will leave the religious and/or spiritual implications to you.

Let's get very basic for a minute. Please write for me a one-sentence description of <u>ethics</u>. Please do this – it's important.

Now write a one-sentence definition of <u>morals</u>.

For purposes of our discussion:

Ethics comprise the rules or standards of personal behavior that are based upon our moral beliefs and values. Morals are those basic beliefs of right and wrong, good versus evil, which govern our conduct.

You know where I'm going with this.

Success, in whatever way you perceive it, is a result of your integrity, that is, how you live up to your principles. However, the pursuit of success in our careers and in our lives exposes us to many situations where our integrity and principles are tested. These tests can come in the form of "opportunities" in which a slight omission of information, a manipulation or deviation from the facts just might land you the job or at least give you an edge over your competition.

One of the reasons it is so difficult to get a handle on whether an action is ethical or not is that ethics as a concept is a great sea of gray. Many times there are no clear-cut, black and white answers. For instance, what if you turned a blind eye to someone harassing another person if you were concerned that you might be attacked yourself or maybe you just didn't want to "get involved"? What if you told a friend a lie because you felt that doing so would save them from certain heartache?

Have you ever cheated on an exam or plagiarized a source and rationalized that "everybody does it"? Have you ever inflated an expense report to get money back when you lost a receipt or felt the company "owes" you? You still signed your name to it...

There are many, many more examples of things such as these in everyday life that may seem insignificant taken singly, but collectively form an ethical cloud over you.

> *TIP: As you transition from academe to career, realize that as the rewards increase so do the risks. As temptations escalate your integrity will be tested continually and only you can determine where the line between ethical and unethical is for you. Live up to that.*

ABOUT LYING

DON'T.

The ethical choice of telling the truth or lying comes up for people every day and especially during the job search and the interview process when you are aspiring to something you want very much.

It's tempting to do whatever you can to make yourself appear more marketable, but that is a slippery slope: Have you "enhanced" certain items on your resume? Sugarcoated the facts about why you left your previous job?

Let me state unequivocally that if you want to achieve success in the job search and don't wish to injure yourself, **NEVER LIE.** Ethical violations, especially those involving lying, are a major cause for firings. Shannon S., the store manager of Target in Santa Rosa, California spoke to one of my marketing classes and told the students that she has to deal with ethical infractions by employees *almost every day.* You will also, so treat the subject seriously, please.

Not lying about anything is important for several reasons. First, from a personal aspect, it is wrong morally and not only reflects on you as a person but also, I believe, can actually work on your personality in a negative way and reduce your effectiveness as a job seeker and interviewee.

From a practical standpoint, if you get caught in a lie — even in a simple matter — the person you lied to will remember it and your trust with that person will be damaged, maybe irrevocably. Basically, they will be trying to protect themselves from you. Nobody likes a liar. Even liars don't like liars because a liar could put them at a disadvantage in a future encounter.

In the job search, some hyperbole is OK, but an outright lie is not. Being caught in one usually brings disaster and you may be branded with this stigma permanently.

Case in Point:

I placed a smart, energetic candidate, Ed L., in a sales position with a major software company in Houston with a reputation for excellent products and for treating its employees well. My candidate, now a new hire, lived in the LA area and had to fly to Texas for two weeks of job orientation and training.

As Ed later lamented to me, during the second week of training two people came to the classroom door and asked the instructor if they could see Ed outside in the hallway. Ed had no idea what was going on until they asked him about his resume. "Ed, you state here that you received a BS in Business Admin from Sacramento State in 1991. We checked with them twice and they said that although you attended classes there for 3-plus years, they have no record of your being awarded a degree. Can you help us understand this?"

Ed anxiously explained that he was six units shy of completing his degree work. His wife got ill during his final semester and he left school to get a job in order to make ends meet. He said that he fully intended to go back and finish the final six units, but he just didn't have the time to go to night school.

Well ... long story short, Ed was fired on the spot, and that evening he was on a plane back to LA to explain to his family why he no longer had the fabulous job.

In Ed's case, his lie was easy to check out. He either had a degree or he didn't. Other exaggerated claims or embellishments can be very hard for the client to check out. So why don't you push things a little to build up your background, you ask? It can't hurt, can it? And the company involved can't really check it out, right?

It's true that most hiring managers can't verify specific data about a former or current employee by calling the company involved. Legally the company may disclose job title and dates of employment. They don't want to be sued by a candidate who lost a job opportunity because of the information they gave about him/her. However, they can say whether or not they would hire you back. What would they say about you?

However, there *are* ways to get specific information through the back door. Here's a case in point when I was with Xerox.

Case in Point:

I got a call from a friend of mine, Bill B., a stockbroker at Merrill Lynch in San Francisco. He asked if I knew a Jake W., who said he was currently employed at Xerox in my office as a sales rep. I told him I did. Bill said that Jake claimed on his resume that he was currently 120% of quota, which would have put him in the upper 25% of sales reps in the branch. Was this true?

Three things worked against Jake in this case. First, he lied. Second, Xerox posted a leader board of all sales reps and where they stood year-to-date on a wall at the branch, visible to everyone. Jake was not 120% of quota nor was he one of the leading sales reps in the branch as he claimed; actually, he was 80% of quota and one of the lowest performers. Third, Bill was a good friend of mine and I trusted him, so I wasn't afraid to give him this information. Xerox would not be implicated in any way. Needless to say, Jake didn't get the job at Merrill.

Hiring managers will do everything they can to find someone in their company who knows you, knows of you, knows someone in your current company, knows a friend of a friend that knows of you. This is how they try to get the real dope on you and to verify anything on your resume or anything you stated in the interview. This "off-the-record," back door fact-checking goes on all the time, and the candidate involved will probably never know about it.

NEVER LIE ABOUT ANYTHING. It's just not worth it. Besides, you have a lot to sell without having to lie. Concentrate on that.

ABOUT LUCK

"I find that the harder I work, the more luck I seem to have."
(Thomas Jefferson)

Luck might be called the consummate wild card in life. In one respect it's unexplainable and elusive. In another it can be said that luck is hard work plus preparedness meeting opportunity. You can't "plan" on having good luck, but it will be essential to your success over the years.

Napoleon expressed his notion of the nature of luck when he was presented with a candidate nominated to become a general officer. The interviewing committee stated that the officer had demonstrated exceptional brilliance in his career, to which Napoleon replied, "Yes I know he is brilliant, but is he lucky?"

The best way to summon a visit from this covetable phantom, I feel, is to take the time to explore who you are, what you value, and what really makes you happy. Leave the outside and online worlds and go to that quiet place within yourself.

As you discover more and more of who you are, you are effectively casting out a baited line into the ocean of the cosmos, and sooner or later you will land a big one in the form of luck. It will probably come as a complete surprise, and sometimes you will only know how lucky you were in a particular situation through the lens of retrospect.

What else attracts "luck" to you? Giving. Giving to someone or something in need has karmic, cosmic power. It's pretty simple: If you want to receive something that's important to you, you must give something, unselfishly and unstintingly. Whatever your take is on this cosmic exchange of good, give it a try. I know that you probably don't have much to give in a material sense right now, but the giving doesn't have to be a material thing. Give of your time, your attention, your positive energy. Offer an encouraging word to some one who is down and out. Be a part of someone else's support group.

Yes, luck comes and goes in mysterious ways, but we do influence it by what we value, how we act, how we think, and how we give.

An example of exceptional luck from my own experience is something I don't often share, but feels appropriate here. This tale of luck revolves around a mistake that was made in good faith, a mistake that changed my life forever.

Case in Point:

I was commissioned as a second lieutenant when I graduated from the University of Illinois in the spring of 1965 and given a two-year leave of absence to pursue a graduate degree at Northern Illinois University. This was at the escalation of the Vietnam War. After I got my Master's in the spring of 1967 and was about to go onto active duty as a second lieutenant, I was presented with what in the Army is called a "dream sheet."

On the dream sheet new officers list where they wanted to be stationed, which could be anywhere in the world. Of course, my buddies put down any plush assignment they could think of, such as Germany, Italy, Japan, Hawaii, anywhere Army troops were stationed (any place other than war zones, of course).

However, the needs of the service really dictated where new second lieutenants would be sent. For every base in Germany or Italy, there were dozens of freezing cold places in the winter, baked-out posts in the summer, places without trees, places that were hot and humid with plenty of mosquitoes, places with way too much rain or snow. You get the idea. And of course there was Vietnam, which had an insatiable appetite for troops at the time — especially green lieutenants. So, I played the dream sheet game and put California as my first choice, Germany as my second, and Italy as my third.

Then came the fateful mistake.

I was supposed to return my personnel packet including the dream sheet to the US Army Administrative Processing Center, a massive office building in St Louis, Missouri. Instead, I inadvertently sent it to the Army offices in the *Pentagon*. In *Washington, D.C.*

Oops!

A few weeks later, during officer basic training, I was notified that I was granted my first choice, California. My company commander during basic, Major G., looked at my orders that read "PSFCA." He said that he had never seen this designation before; neither had I. We found out that not only was

I going to California, but to one of the most prestigious posts in the country: PSFCA ... that is, The Presidio of San Francisco.

When I arrived in SF at Headquarters XV US Army Corps to report for duty, the Sergeant Major in charge asked, *Are you sure, Sir, that you're in the right place?* There were no other second lieutenants there at the time, mostly light colonels, bird colonels and generals. Senior officers went to the Presidio to retire. Sure I was sure, I replied, and nervously presented my orders.

Apparently my personnel packet, including the notorious dream sheet, drew attention: whoever received it at the Pentagon must have assumed that it must be from someone important, or somebody who knows someone important and so processed the paperwork without question. The point is that it got special attention even when it shouldn't have.

Luck had everything to do with it. Being stationed in California changed my life forever because I decided to stay in the Bay Area, raise a family there and pursue my career(s) there. Without this amazing piece of luck, my life would have taken a completely different path.

Luck is an essential ingredient to success in life. Support its presence with some positive vibes and someday it will walk up and shake hands with you, probably when you least expect it.

COLD-CALLING (or ... IF YOU CAN'T GET AN INTERVIEW APPOINTMENT, JUST GO THERE)

This is not a contradiction. It means just what it says — Go there!

Go to the company of your choice without an appointment. Just get up off your butt and go. By doing this unannounced, you will be making what is known in the sales game as a **"cold-call."** You walk in the door ... you don't know them ... they don't know you. It's cold all right, downright freezing and stomach-churning. But it's also an act of courage, and it might just get you an interview on the spot.

If you can't find out who the hiring manager is at a company you want to work for, before you mail or deliver your personal information packet (as covered in Chapter 2), go to the company and ask to speak to the hiring manager for the advertised job opening.

If that's not possible, then try to get to any manager, tell them that you want to work there and ask for five minutes to tell them why. You will be amazed at how often they will stop in their tracks and listen. Have your "pitch" well-rehearsed and be certain that you have a copy of your resume (two is better) with you. Have your pitch timed and stick to *two minutes*, unless they keep asking you questions. If they do, just roll with it and stay until you can get a next step, if you can get one. Be prepared to leave your information packet behind.

The **cold-call** is one of the most difficult things to do in sales ... to my mind, *the* most difficult. Most non-sales people won't do it, and in my three-decades-plus of selling experience, I know that many sales people don't do it. Companies train sales people in cold-call techniques and require sales people to do it because the cold-call is an important source of new business, i.e., it brings new money into the company. The techniques of cold-calling are neither complex nor difficult to understand; the difficulty is in finding the guts to do it.

I also believe that cold-calling has become somewhat of a lost art, mainly because of the Internet and its ease of use in broadcasting messages to target markets. Tight security employed at all large companies today and even in many of the small ones also impedes getting past (or even to) the reception desk.

But there are ways around security if you are smart enough and bold enough.

> TIP: *Leaving your personal packet of information, even if it's with a security guard or receptionist, is one example of how to get in. Even if you are told that you must fill out an application online and they can't let you in without an appointment, they just might call someone to come get the packet, or perhaps deliver it themselves. If you're creative in how you make your packet of information look, including a manager's name conspicuously on the cover, if possible, will almost certainly get into the hands of a manager of some kind. If you can't get a manager's name, address it to the "Manager of the Accounting Department" or whatever. In any case, you just got one hell of a lot more attention from your target company than by just using the Internet.*

As I've stated before, companies receive thousands, tens of thousands of resumes and applications online. What distinguishes yours from anyone else's? All you have to do is sit back and wait for the responses to pour in, right? Wrong. Your inertia will produce exactly the same result as what you put out ... Nothing. You can lull yourself into thinking you have done due diligence and connected with countless potential employers simply through online postings, but if you don't follow up an Internet "cattle call" with a personal effort like a **cold-call**, *you'll* be left out in the cold.

Managers are impressed with people who cold-call, especially when they are promoting themselves. It shows initiative, gumption, spunk, drive, courage, and maybe most of all, creativity, depending on what kind of support materials you bring with you, and how you do your initial "pitch." It also shows that you are extremely interested in their company.

Case in Point:

Two female students from one of my seminars at SSU, due to graduate in May of 2011, took it upon themselves to do something extra in the very difficult job market of 2010-11. The university had projected that approximately 40% of graduating students for both years would not have a career job when they received their degrees. This situation was unprecedented at SSU as well as at many other universities and colleges around California and the country.

These two young women went out on their own and set out for northern California's Sonoma County wine country. The specific area they chose was the Valley of the Moon, noted not only for its many highly-rated wineries but also for its breathtaking beauty. They visited five wineries in one afternoon and received *two job offers*. Security wasn't a problem as far as accessing the right managers because they chose smaller wineries that made public access fairly easy. Even though the managers involved were working at the time, they took the time to listen to these gutsy students

Taylor Swift is another excellent example of cold-calling success. "Sixty Minutes" did a profile on the singer and her phenomenal rise to stardom and business success, on November 20, 2011. The story pointed out that when she was unknown and just starting out, she created a CD of her own music. Taylor and her mother went to Nashville, the capital of country music, and Taylor personally went into the radio stations in town, made her pitch, and left a CD with all of them. The rest is music business history. This sensational young woman did exactly what my students did: made cold calls with support materials (**the information packet**). It works.

The power of the cold-call: If you have the courage to do it, under the right circumstances you just went to the head of the interviewing line when you walked through the door.

CHAPTER 8
"WHAT IFS"

"I am always doing things I can't do;
that's how I get to do them." (Pablo Picasso)

In summary, the main goal of the interview process is to get an offer letter. The second most important goal, aside from an offer letter, is to get a "next step" in the process to insure that your candidacy is still alive and well.

But ... **WHAT IF...** ?

What if ... it's a committee interview?

Occasionally, you will be asked to participate in an interview with more than one person. This is called the **committee interview** and it has a different dynamic than the one-on-one experience. Non-profits, public and government institutions tend to use this type of interview process more than do private, fast-paced for-profit companies. Interviewing committees can be as small as two or as large as eight to ten people. Any more than that and it becomes more of an inquisition than an interview (US Congressional committee meetings are an extreme example of this).

However, the number of interviewers and format of the committee interview usually follow strict procedural guidelines. The members of the committee will provide a spectrum of various functions within the organization, from most to least influential as far as the value of their final vote on your hiring. Some people will be asked to serve on the interviewing committee even though they won't work with you if you are hired. So you have an artificial situation — a conventional interview — wrapped around another artificial situation, the committee interview, to make things even more complex than you could have imagined.

There is a powerful dynamic at play in the committee interview because of the nature of the internal competitiveness of committee members. It's understandable to be apprehensive about the committee interview; however, you are just as likely to have members that support your candidacy as not. And although there is the pressure of appearing before multiple interviewers at once, most committee interviews are cordial affairs. How you are treated will largely depend upon how powerful your hiring manager is within the organization. The more influential or powerful, the better for you.

Since you probably can't get information in advance on internal politics (which tend to be complex), it's probably best that you just concentrate on presenting your professional best, have good energy, make good eye contact with each committee member as they question you and be respectful to *everyone*. This is one of the few places in life where you do have to try to please everyone because each one represents a vote for or against you.

Institutions are generally aware of the artificial nature and the ensuing negative possibilities of the committee interview and, if they are well managed, have taken steps to eliminate them.

For instance, sometimes you will face an interviewing committee that uses standardized questions that are written up in advance. This is done in order to ensure that committee members remain impartial, that is, to show no favoritism to any single candidate. Unfortunately, this may come across as calculated, formal and inflexible.

You must be on your toes and find any opportunity to reveal your true self within the canned questions. Be very sure to have good questions to ask in order to use their answers to bring out your strengths in the form of benefits to them. Once again, your objective is to get a job offer.

What if … you're waiting for the interview and get nervous?

Waiting for an interview can be nerve-wracking, especially true when you have to wait more than a few minutes. While waiting, you need a calm place to go to — not down the hall or in a shadowy corner of the reception area, but *within yourself*. Breathe deeply and focus inward. It's called "getting centered."

Here's a personal scenario I revisit.

Case in Point:

When I was the Xerox National Account Manager for Bechtel, I had an exceptional experience one day while waiting to see a senior-level executive. I forget now what I was trying to sell at the time, but the point is, effectively I was waiting for an "interview" with an important decision maker.

When I arrived at the reception area, there was another salesman waiting for his appointment with the same executive. Several minutes passed in silence and then the other guy, the receptionist, and I started conversing. An article in a magazine on the table in front of us triggered a conversation about death and dying, of all things.

I can't remember how this conversation progressed to the point that the other salesman, in a very open and peaceful manner, began to relate how he went through a near-death experience himself. He said that in the previous year, he had been undergoing open-heart surgery and for some reason was able to hear what was going on in the operating room. Near the end of the operation, after he had been sewn up, he could hear one of the medical team exclaim, "We're losing him!" The salesman said that despite the thought that he was about to die, he had felt a great calmness, total serenity, and had a clear thought that everything was OK. The last words he heard in the operating room, he said, were the surgeon's, "Open him up!"

What I remember about this man was his composure. He was centered, alert, with good energy. He wasn't trying to impress us. He just told his story clearly, without overstatement or embellishment. The receptionist and I just sat in silence, transfixed.

I remember his words, his calmness, his certitude, and most important, how he made me *feel*. In the many years since that day, I have tried to duplicate this awareness in myself, and I don't think that I have quite gotten there — yet. I know that it's there inside me, as it is in all of us, hidden under layers of conditioning like layers of paint to be peeled away.

From a practical standpoint I know that this calmness and assurance would make me an exceptional salesman. It would dwarf all training, personality, and force of will that normally are possessed by truly great salespeople. But more than that, I have been reaching for the core of myself, where the keys to greatness in any endeavor reside in all of us. This process is a timeless journey. I believe that the attainment of this calm, centered state gets closer every step of the way we take in our journey to know ourselves, if our motives are sincere.

The focal point of this wonderful encounter was how this man made me feel. I have come to learn in my own endeavors that people will remember a little of what you say to them, a little more of what you do, but they will remember a lot about *how you made them feel.*

One effective way for me has been to find a quiet space and visualize something or a situation that calms me. Visualizations can be very powerful tools, mainly because they help us recall positive experiences in our lives and help to reinforce belief in ourselves. This belief in ourselves and our abilities can be summed up in two words, "I can!"

The Roman philosopher Virgil explained it succinctly, "They can because they think they can." This powerful thought has been the subject of philosophical discussion over centuries, paraphrased in countless works of literature and acts of courage in history. It works. If so many great minds have recognized this truth, I suggest that you do, too, and apply it wholeheartedly to your search activities.

TIP: Find something that makes you feel good inside. Then create your quiet place within, where calmness resides, and you will find your most effective, assured self. Visualize the interview going well and you being made a job offer!

What if ... you're naturally shy?

During the interview process, you will have to confront a few demons that relate to nervousness, shyness, or outright fear. In my career as a headhunter I have had lots of experience with people who have struggled with shyness. Situational shyness or nervousness can occur for many people when they find themselves in unfamiliar territory, such as social situations or when they are in the spotlight ... all the more so for those with an introverted personality.

The job interview is one of the most challenging and unforgiving of these situations.

Lack of confidence, or even the *appearance* of lack of confidence, is a major reason for failure in the job interview. The interview is not a place to be shy or retiring. Realize that through your preparation, education, and hopefully some prior work experience, you have a lot to offer. You must be convinced that you have the qualities that the employer is looking for and be unashamed to state them both as strengths about you and also as benefits to them.

How do you overcome your shyness? There are probably as many ways to do this as there are shy personalities, but you must find one that works for *you*. Review the material in Chapter 4.

> *TIP: A psychologist who helped me through a hard time in my life also guided me through a process to help when things around you are very active/stressful, and you suddenly are overcome with fear. The process is this: "Stop. Take a deep breath. Consider. Take Action." The "consider" part is the place where you can recall the visualization that you created earlier. If you don't think that this process wouldn't apply to you and isn't worth your effort to give it a try, consider the fact that this process is taught in basic training for US Navy Seals.*

What if ... things start to go bad in the interview?

At some point in your few-to-many years of interviewing you will encounter a situation during the interview that gives you a feeling that things aren't going well. The atmosphere has turned sour and tense, for whatever reason. Any of the following could contribute to such a situation:

- *Miscommunication of any kind.* This can take the form of awkward conversation, a faux pas on your part, an answer from you that was dumb, inaccurate, or incorrect.

- *A feeling that you just haven't connected.* This means bad chemistry or no chemistry has been established.

- *Poor Body Language.* Previously described in Chapter 4.

- *Early Wrap-up.* The interviewer starts to wrap things up after 15 minutes or so.

- *Interviewer boredom or inattention.* This generally means that the job has already been filled, or they think that you are not qualified for the job.

Regardless of the reason for a bad or awkward atmosphere, you are in trouble and have to act fast. The most effective thing to do at this point is to state positively and directly that you apologize that the communication between you is not going well (even if it's not your fault) and that you would like to restart things. Doing this shows the interviewer that you are a cut above the average candidate, that you are observant, that you have courage, and that you probably have the makings of a good manager.

Most candidates won't do this. If the interviewer has any sense of professionalism they will level with you, acknowledge the miscommunication and hopefully will explain more clearly what their agenda really is. If the job has already been filled, or if you have a negative disqualifier (such as a GPA that's too low for this position), at least you won't be wasting your time further. You will also have taken a giant step forward in improving your interviewing skills.

Case in Point:

A student of mine, Jeremiah A., who had just graduated and was in the early stages of interviewing, found himself in a situation during an interview in which things just weren't going well. It was a committee interview — five people — and Jeremiah emailed me that he did just what I recommended. He asked for a restart. He got the job and a committee member told him after the interview that they were impressed at how well he handled himself.

Courage displayed on your part during an interview will usually impress.

What if ... you get a bad interviewer?

Once in a while you will encounter an interviewer who is not very good at it, is filling in for someone else, or is outright incompetent or prejudiced. This won't happen very often, but when it does it will be obvious after a few minutes into the interview.

Here are some clues to look for: Novice or incompetent interviewers often are not prepared. They either won't have your paperwork or will fumble around looking for it, or won't have read it at all. They will tend to speak in generalities or banalities and may even take on a pontificating tone.

Inept or company "yes men" will descend into the verbal black hole called "corporate-speak," using such hackneyed phrases as *point with pride... we're focusing on our core competencies* (or) *our company culture & values... we're blowing it out... we're rightsizing, re-org'ing, re-engineering... filling the pipeline... our secret is synergy* (or synergistic anything)... *we need to redouble our efforts...* and the inevitable *our employees are our best asset*, etc., etc. You probably have heard most of them already.

If someone uses a lot of phrases like these during the interview or acts in a self-important or condescending manner, you can be fairly sure that the interviewer is a corporate hack who won't take chances or be upfront with you. If you view this interview as important and want to get a shot at another interview with this company, be polite. Do your best to get a next step in one of the ways we discussed previously, and focus on progressing to an interview with the hiring manager.

If you can't confirm a next step with this interviewer, go over his head directly to the hiring manager. This is a risky tactic, but at this point you have nothing to lose. If you then get a second interview like the first, hold your nose, and watch where you step on the way out. You now have good evidence that you wouldn't be happy working in a place that pays its employees in bull**.

What if ... you've been fired or laid off?

The notion that a candidate should have a job while looking for another one is a basic tenet in recruiting. The candidate not only appears more desirable to a prospective employer but also is less likely to feel desperate.

The exception, of course, is if you are still in school. Since the target audience of this book is juniors, seniors and recent college graduates who are looking for their first or second career job, I should note that being in school or having just graduated is the only time in your career when not having a job while interviewing *will not hurt you or your chances of securing a good job*. In the future, employers will look on you much more favorably as a candidate if you have a job while you are interviewing than if you don't.

If you have already graduated, had a job but lost it, you must decide how you will disclose that fact before you sit down in an interview with anyone. When they discover early on that you were laid off, got fired or that you quit, they will ask you to explain why, before they spend any more time with you.

Let me say that you must be prepared to deal with this situation right out of the box in the interview process or the company won't give you the attention you deserve. My best advice is to have an answer prepared that explains clearly, openly, and truthfully what happened to put you out of your former job and into your current circumstances. If this is well thought out on your part and expressed in a positive way, especially if you can turn it into a growth experience, you will most likely eliminate any concerns, start to earn their respect, and begin the interview process on a very positive note.

I was fired/laid off three times. You probably will also be fired at least once. In fact, one theory on being fired suggests that if you're forty years old and haven't been fired at least once, you're probably very lucky or you just aren't being aggressive enough in executing your job responsibilities and taking chances. I subscribe to that theory ... within reason.

The word "fired" is one of the most euphemized words in the English language: laid-off, downsized, right-sized, canned, shit-canned, terminated, made redundant, got your notice, dismissed, discharged, cut, sacked, whacked, shot, pink-slipped, dumped, axed. Or ... you lost your job through merger, acquisition, bankruptcy, or because of budget cuts. Navigating through the corporate or institutional doublespeak, whatever the cause or whatever you call it, you lost your job.

There are clues that will give you a good idea of when to update your resume and re-hone your interviewing skills.

If a company has trouble making payroll, or has to borrow to make payroll, or can't get a loan to make payroll, start looking. If cash flow takes a serious hit for whatever reason, if order volume drops significantly, if the owners start to fight over how the business should operate, start calling people in your network.

Likewise, if there is a merger or acquisition and your company is on the acquired end of things, start meeting with your support group on an active basis.

During the early stages of a merger or acquisition, you should get some initial clues that something is afoot. This is the time when the corporate cavalcade of clichés commences. "We're dedicated to excellence, we're committed to future growth, we believe that this merger positions us well for the future, we're committed to quality products and services," etc. You will also probably get a statement from company officials declaring that "nothing will change," or that "the way we do business won't change." If you hear either of these last two statements or something similar, the spin doctors are at work.

Notice that there is no mention of employees or their future in any of the above statements. Corporate types are good at avoiding or at clouding any meaningful discussion of the specific key issues of any change. The reason is that they fear the wholesale resignations that could occur in a short period of time: the company could be seriously hurt if even a few key individuals were to leave suddenly, so they equivocate, obfuscate and exaggerate.

After the official announcements are made, a period of silence will ensue. When the layoffs do occur they usually happen suddenly and feel like a car wreck. It could occur as soon as one month and more likely around four to six months after the announcement of the merger/acquisition and after management has had time to see who really is redundant.

If you are one of the unfortunates to get your notice, it's important to understand how the environment will change for you. Management will become more distant, impersonal, and even cold to those leaving. Some employees who thought that they couldn't possibly be cut, get cut. You could be treated as if you never worked there. It all becomes strictly business, and the company chemistry, as far as you're concerned, changes completely.

Re-read your employment agreement immediately, if you haven't already. It's all you have now, and the company doesn't have to give you anything else. You will be very upset and will take all of this personally, but keep a clear head. Thoughts of suing them might occur to you at some point, but unless you have suffered egregious harm and can prove it with hard evidence, forget about it. It's not worth your valuable time and the effort involved will drain you. I've seen the futility of this suing process twice, and it reminds me of an old Chinese proverb: "If you seek revenge, dig two graves."

Getting laid off is beyond your control. But getting the real "F" — getting fired — for reasons such as poor performance, poor attendance, or a persistently poor attitude, for instance, can be a valuable, though painful personal wakeup call. What are you going to learn from this?

Whatever happened to make you jobless, take a day or two off to calm down and get through some of the pain of loss, reflect on what you will take from the experience and *move on*. Something good is waiting for you around the next corner. Really. But before you turn that corner, it's back to your action plan, to your network and your support group.

Being laid off because of a downsizing, right-sizing, a re-engineering of the company, being made redundant, or any other of the many corporate euphemisms you may come across, is easier to explain than that you were fired or that you quit. Being fired raises a red flag for potential employers, as can walking away from a job. Walking away, as long as it was done with respect and courtesy, can be dealt with in a straightforward manner. It happens all the time.

Being fired, however, carries negative baggage with it until it is explained properly. You must always tell the truth about what really happened, even if it makes you feel uncomfortable or embarrassed.

Being fired hurts. It's a blow to self-esteem and it's something that has to be recovered from, sometimes fast. But it's a well-known fact among recruiters and good managers that not all firings were deserved. Some were blunders perpetrated by incompetent or corrupt management on good people. Some were done because of association with others who deserved to be fired and took the innocent with them. Others occurred because of a stupid mistake committed by an otherwise good employee, who will never make that mistake again.

It is my personal belief that, after seeing many firings during thirty-three years in industry and ten in academe, if you haven't been fired at least once in your career you probably weren't pushing (for ethically sound reasons, of course!) the success envelope aggressively enough. As I've said before, I was fired three times during my working years and in all three cases I went on to something better and something that paid *more*.

> *"I am never discouraged because every wrong attempt*
> *discarded is a step forward."*
> *(Thomas Alva Edison)*

FINAL THOUGHTS

> *"If you do follow your bliss you put yourself on a kind of track*
> *that has been there all the while, waiting for you, and the life*
> *that you ought to be living is the one you are living. When you*
> *can see that, you begin to meet people who are in your field*
> *of bliss, and they open doors to you.*
>
> *I say, follow your bliss and don't be afraid, and doors will*
> *open where you didn't know they were going to be."*
>
> *(Joseph Campbell)*[10]

As I've said previously, the job search is also a search for self.

The evaluation process one goes through in examining career choices, where you will work, companies you will work for, and especially how well you will interview will reveal a lot about who you are as a person. It's about discovering things about *you* that were there all along but required a journey of self-exploration to bring them out.

However, this isn't just about one long journey where we have to wait for the final finish line to learn who we are. Meaningful journeys can be as short as

---

10   Campbell, Joseph. <u>Joseph Campbell and The Power of Myth with Bill Moyers</u>. Anchor Books, 1991.

one day, one hour, that together add up to the self-awareness, the field of bliss Joseph Campbell speaks of so eloquently.

The interview process is both riddled with rules and procedures that must be understood and followed and also emotionally challenging because it compels us to look at the very core of ourselves. I have endeavored, in the analyses, procedures and guidelines offered in this book, to help clarify a complex topic and make it cogent and accessible.

Only you will know if I have succeeded.

It is my hope that I have helped you in your journey to carry out a successful job search, to interview well, and to help you make the transition from successful student to successful professional.

I am glad to have been your personal headhunter, even for a short while, on your journey.

APPENDIX A

THE HIRING FILTER AND HIRING PROCESS CHECKLIST

As stated in Chapter 5, an excellent client of mine in the rapidly growing high-tech sector of the nineties created two simple tools to assist managers, especially new managers and recent college graduates, in interviewing new candidates. The company's business was growing rapidly, they were hiring lots of people as fast as they could, and there was no time to train managers in basic interviewing techniques.

The tools are simple and straightforward, but they give you an insight as to what management felt was important to explore when interviewing a prospective hire. I was given these tools by management to help me better understand their hiring process.

The tools are called the Hiring Filter and the Hiring Process Checklist. Read the questions, develop general responses to them, and rehearse!

THE HIRING FILTER

As you consider a candidate, consider the following qualities. This is not an exhaustive list, but without these qualities, a candidate will not succeed at (our company):

- **Passion**

  - Does this person really get excited about their work and their team?

- Tell me about what really gets you excited/invigorated at work?

- Give me an example of something you feel passionately about.

- **Willingness to Risk**

  - Will this person stick his or her neck out to do the right thing?

  - Tell me about something you believed deeply about at work and what you did about it.

  - What's the biggest risk you took at work?

- **Ethical**

  - Will this person do the right thing for the business, the customer, and the team?

  - How far would you go to accomplish an objective *(use example)* or do what you believe in?

  - Sometimes business requires bending some rules. Tell me about some times you have done that.

- **Adaptable**

  - Can this individual adapt to change by committing despite reservations?

  - Give me an example of a time when things changed and you really didn't agree with it...What did you do?

- **Final checks before you make an offer (or move to the next step):**

  - Is this person better than you?

  - Are you prepared to be accountable for hiring this person?

  - Are you passionate about hiring this person? This person will reflect on you.

THE HIRING PROCESS CHECKLIST

- **Know What You Need**

- Operations – Budget Approved?

- Operations – Job complete with job description?

- **How Do You Find the Right Person?**

  - Work with Employment Services/HR to create a recruiting plan.

  - Over 50% of our hires come from internal referrals.

- **Interview Candidates**

  - Create a team interview plan. Don't leave this to chance!

  - Keep things moving. Limit the interview cycle.

  - Make sure your team is prepared to cover the right topics.

- **Select Your Finalists**

  - Work fast. Collect data from your team.

  - Check references (not just the ones on their list!).

  - Keep the candidates engaged.

- **Make that offer**

  - Get the OK from your VP or Director.

  - Employment Services will create your offer letter.

  - Move quickly! Don't let a good one get away!

- **Get (the candidate's) Signature**

  NOW, the real work begins!!!

.

APPENDIX B
THE TELEPHONE INTERVIEW

The main purpose of the telephone or videoconference interview is to secure a live face-to-face interview.

It's pretty easy to have a conversation with a prospective employer on the phone, right? Not really. If you are discourteous or mumble or seem awkward on the phone, it will go against you. If you don't have important information, such as the job description, at your fingertips, you will probably strike out. If you use language that was appropriate for the dorm, fraternity, sorority or pub, you will peg yourself immediately as immature. If you have a recorded phone message that is similar to the above, or is any way not businesslike, you may not get a callback. Save slang for private conversations.

The phone interview will likely be a short one. Nobody gets hired over the phone, so what the person calling you is most likely interested in is checking for disqualifiers. In the recruiting jargon, you're being screened.

Screening questions assess your overall qualifications and profile against the basic requirements of the job. You may be asked, "Will you graduate this June or December. No? Sorry we bothered you." "Can you clarify something (anything) on your resume?" "You didn't show a GPA on your resume. What is it?" "Your resume says that you interned at ABC Company last year; who did you report to there? What did you do there? What results did you produce?" "What is your experience with creating spreadsheets?"

The person calling is probably an assistant or an HR staffer who is checking out certain items on your resume that the hiring manager wants to know about in advance, to verify something or to gather more information about you.

The call may simply be to set up a face-to-face interview, in which case you have achieved your chief objective. Make sure to be enthusiastic but don't gush, and write down the name and number of the person who just called and confirm the day and time of the interview as well as the name of the interviewer.

Finally, be polite and businesslike but end the call as quickly as you can; don't provide information the screener doesn't ask for, or ask any complex questions. Think of it as an interview with the IRS; you don't want to say or do anything that could jeopardize the upcoming interview you have just scored. To my mind, lengthy phone interviews can be dangerous. You can't get hired over the phone, but you sure can get eliminated as a candidate.

However, sometimes in-depth phone interviews are a necessity. These may occur because of schedule conflicts on the part of the interviewer, or because of a long distance between you.

> TIP: If the interview is for a scheduled time, make sure you will not be interrupted and are in a place that is quiet. Take the call over a land-line, which normally has better audio, and the battery won't run out! Also, have the job description and blank paper with pen in case you want to jot something down to reference later in the interview.

If their offices are in another city many miles away, a videoconference could be set up if you have the proper equipment. They may ask if you have a Skype account. If you don't have one now, get one. It's free, and it's easy to set up.

When you do your set-up for Skype, be sure you have a good background when you are on camera. Keep it conservative. A blank wall is fine. No posters about paratroopers with skulls and a motto that says "Death From Above." It may have looked great in your dorm room, but not here. Have all pertinent information at your fingertips and writing material to take notes. Dress as you would for a face-to-face meeting and have a friend check how you look on camera in advance of your interview.

Phone interviews are not and never will be a substitute for a face-to-face interview; a videoconferencing call is better but still not the same. And even if you wind up having a smashingly good phone conversation because of your phenomenal telephonic personality, you still have to go through a real live interview at some point anyway.

Good chemistry most likely cannot be established over the phone. However, because of the limitations of a voice-only encounter, seemingly small errors that would be ignored in a face-to-face meeting can add up to something more serious, that is, a bad feeling on the part of the caller. This vague bad feeling is everyone's nemesis. It's our old enemy, bad chemistry.

TIP: If you are forced by circumstance to have a lengthy phone or videoconference interview, your main objective remains: You must close for a face-to-face meeting. Follow the guidelines for interviewing, as described in Chapters 3 and 4, especially about benefit statements. Respond professionally to all questions put to you, but at the end you must close for a face-to-face. "Mr. Jones, you mentioned that you will be back in town on the 23rd; can we meet at your offices on that day? You're booked up on that day? How about the 24th? I've enjoyed our conversation very much and would like to meet you in person."

APPENDIX C
THE INTERNET

"Men have become the tools of their tools... Our inventions are wont to be pretty toys, which distract our attention from serious things. They are but an unproved means to an unimproved end, an end which it was already but too easy to arrive at..."
(Henry David Thoreau)

Thoreau made this observation 167 years ago.[11]

THE INTERNET, MULTI-TASKING AND COGNITIVE LEARNING — PROS & CONS

The Internet is one of the most useful tools ever invented. It's right up there with the printing press, radio, refrigeration, the automobile and television. But it is just a tool, and much to our dismay we have allowed it to become a good deal more than that. In many respects, it controls us rather than the other way around. This is especially critical to counteract in the interview process where concentration and interpersonal communication skills are paramount.

In his latest work, <u>The Shallows: What the Internet Is Doing To Our Brains,</u>[12] Pulitzer Prize nominee Nicholas Carr examines the human side of Internet-related things and comes up with some unsettling conclusions. "When we go online, we're following scripts written by others, algorithmic instructions

---

11   Thoreau, Henry David. Journal entry, 1845, <u>The Journal, 1837-1861.</u> Daniel Searls, ed. New York Review Books, 2009.

12   Carr, Nicholas. <u>The Shallows: What the Internet Is Doing To Our Brains.</u> WW Norton & Company, 2010.

that few of us would be able to understand even if the hidden codes were revealed to us." In other words, he argues that we're letting others do our thinking for us. These "scripts" can be amazingly useful as tools, Carr says, but they can also stifle our creativity by hypnotizing us and numbing us into "dependence and routine."[13] You might even say that in some respects we become Internet junkies.

Tools other than the Internet, or tools in association with the Web, can have an additional negative effect on our ability to think independently, productively, and creatively. Multi-tasking is the culprit here, and it has several accessories to its misdemeanors. Any intelligent device, whether it has an "*i*" in front of its name or not, is merely a support device, i.e., iPhones, iPads, iClouds, Kindles, etc. In an article in the New York Times, Phyllis Korkki writes, "As workers add more electronic devices, websites, software programs and apps to their arsenals, there is a point at which efficiency and satisfaction suffer. More devices can lead to more multi-tasking, which though viewed by many as a virtue has been shown to interfere with concentration."[14]

I would add that it's students as well as workers that are subject to this multi-tasking phenomenon, and that deep reflective thought and creativity also suffer.

So, students and workers alike are facing what I call a distraction dilemma that forces them to choose among information delivery devices within a narrow band of time, and increasingly multi-taskers are aware that there is a price to be paid for doing this, yet are at a loss over what to do about it.

It seems to me that multi-tasking with a variety of electronic devices that probably also includes access to the Internet causes a lack of focus in our lives today. In its acute form, lack of focus or *focus futility*, as I call it, puts us in a position that is similar to wearing a pair of glasses or contact lenses with the wrong prescription. In this kind of world, bad decisions are more likely to be made.

---

13   Ibid.

14   Korkki, Phyllis. "The Year of the Multi-tasker's Revenge." New York Times 31 Dec. 2011.

Being "on" all of the time has a mental fatigue factor associated with it. Try walking all day without sitting down; fatigue is bound to set in and with it, reduced efficiency.

A factor that exacerbates all of this is the quicksilver nature of technology. Technological changes happen rapidly and frequently and must be learned on the fly in many cases, unless you are lucky enough to work for a company that re-trains you regularly.

It seems to me that this scenario can create a technology anxiety: *Am I using all the latest and greatest stuff, or am I falling further behind, just ahead of the rampaging tech-savy herd rushing up behind me?* New apps for smart devices are introduced every week, even every day. There are many thousands of them, and it's hard to keep up.

So what's the way out of this Internet-induced, *"iDevice"* multi-tasking dilemma? One way is to focus on your field of endeavor, that is, on what you love to do. These new apps and devices can offer you a great deal of freedom, flexibility, and time-savings, if you can control them. Once again, it comes down to your managing the tools, not the other way around. If used properly with your personality type, the work structure you are comfortable in, and your capacity for endurance and concentration, they can provide a basis for stimulating your creativity. As you know by now Creativityland is the place where big payouts in business occur.

But first you must take a break from this world of stress and fatigue, and re-connect with yourself and others who will support you.

> *TIP: There is at least one way to mitigate the tension endemic to multi-tasking and the electronic device tsunami that feeds it. Getting back to nature seems to work effectively. Numerous psychological studies conducted since the 1980s show that spending time in a quiet natural setting far from the madding crowd contributes significantly to tension reduction, better memory and improved learning ability.*

What's the net (pun intended) of all of this? Don't let your computer, or iPad, iPhone, or anything related to the Internet, program *you*. Don't lose your ability to think harder and better. Growth in personal thinking ability is essential to your continued success, because it will determine how creative you will be, and ultimately how much you will make in whatever career that you choose.

Technology can become an escape mechanism. Better to escape your Internet jail cell and use the technology to support your efforts to meet people *face-to-face*. That's where the real action is. Action that will lead to your next job.

FEED YOUR CREATIVITY

A combination of social interaction, self-reflection, meditation in quiet time and connecting with nature form a powerful mix that feeds creativity. Give your subconscious mind just a few minutes a day to compile all the data you have been processing through your senses. New ideas and new thoughts will bubble up like magic, as Bob Dylan has suggested happened to him when he wrote some of his best songs. When asked where he got the idea for a line of lyrics that he wrote, Dylan replied that he didn't know where that came from... "I just wrote it down." Can you explain where your last creative idea came from? Probably not, but it came to you all the same.

> *TIP: Make quiet time a part of your day, even if it's for 15 minutes. In the hubbub of our exhaustingly active world today, you may find this difficult to do. Endless reasons not to seek out quiet time will occur to you. The struggle will be worth it, because in the quiet place you will find your creativity, and this will lead to your success.*

Go into partnership with your subconscious mind in the quiet place. This partnership is your creativity source, and it's the creativity that makes you a standout problem-solver that employers want. Getting results makes them successful, too, and everyone involved makes money.

We're the only creatures on the planet that have the great gift of the subconscious mind. Take advantage of it.

SOCIAL MEDIA AND NETWORKING

When you are using FaceBook, Twitter, or texting, you're not socializing in the true sense of the word. You're interacting with a robot, which delivers your messages. There is no true-life interaction there. It's artificial.

The robot is extremely effective in delivering data. But you're being robbed of a rich social encounter that is face-to-face communication. Phone conversations, though not face-to-face, are still much more *sociable* than email, texting, tweeting or online chatter.

Why is this important? In order to get a good job you must be effective in face-to-face encounters. It has always been that way and always will be. The robot can help you get a job interview, but it can't interview for you. Like it or not, you must do that for yourself.

> *TIP: After each job search session out there, ask yourself, "How has what I did today helped me get a job? What new information did I get today that will help me in my next interview?" A successful salesperson asks every day, "Will this specific activity lead directly to my getting an order?" If not, eliminate it for now.*

Leave the Web behind for hours at a time, and hone your face-to-face real life socializing skills. It will be hard to get a good job without them. My own success and personal happiness are related to the amount of time I have spent *off* the Internet. The Internet is an enormously useful tool, but there's no *there* there: Human beings are social animals and live social action is where the best of creativity is nurtured.

SOCIAL MEDIA SITES – POTENTIAL RED FLAGS

If you haven't done so already, clean up your social media sites today, RIGHT NOW.

Most potential employers will check these out, and what was once cool or cute could now be cause for rejection. Yes, I know you have put filters on these sites so only your "friends" will have access. But suppose that you have done very well interviewing with a particular company, and you have given them your references and they are checking you out. They may ask if they may have access to your Facebook account in order to get more familiar with who you are. What are you going to do, say No? Saying No is not an option for you if you want to go to work for this company because it would raise a red flag for them.

Eliminate anything and everything from every social networking site that could possibly be viewed as immature, unprofessional, or worse. If you're not sure about something being offensive, ask someone from your support group to help you, someone who has been in the business world for a while. The carefree days of just about "anything goes" on the Internet are over for you.

Even if a company doesn't feel the need to check out your social media while you are in the interview process, there is another important reason why you should remove material that could hurt you. When you post something on the Internet, it could go worldwide in a few seconds *but it will linger for a lifetime.*

The example of New York Congressman Anthony Weiner, a career fiasco that made national headlines for weeks during June 2011 is a sobering example. As you probably know, he accidently sent out embarrassing, compromising data about his sexual life, and it cost him not only his congressional seat but also his political future. And it all happened in less than a second, the blink of an eye, a moment to click on the fatally wrong button.

Weiner may be a smart man, but he is also very arrogant, and that was in large part his downfall. I have seen this many, many times over the years where arrogance creates a type of stupidity that derails brilliance. I know that you are technically savvy. Just please don't get self-important about it and kill yourself.

Also, suppose that one of your once "friends" is no longer a friend but while he was a "friend" he downloaded images of you shitfaced and half-dressed at a post-victory football party two years ago. Now this person hears that you just got a job with ABC Company and he forwards these images to your new company HR just for the hell of it, or maybe to get back at you for something. Do you need the kind of grief that could come from this? An old rule of thumb about personal behavior is this: would it be OK for this graphic to appear on the front page of tomorrow's newspaper?

While you're at it, *change your email address(es) or phone answering messages that smack of anything unprofessional.* An email address such as "bigstickdude@aol.com" will hurt you in more ways than one. With all respect to Teddy Roosevelt and your sexual prowess, the big stick approach is not viable here. You've seen the email addresses and heard the voicemail phone answers that I'm referring to, so you know what to do.

It was not uncommon in the past for some companies to hire a researcher, even a private investigator, to check up on someone before a job offer was made. Today the private investigators come in sophisticated software products that go well beyond Google to reveal sensitive things about you, such as your credit rating, DUIs, and other infractions, misdemeanors or felony convictions.

FACEBOOK, LINKED-IN, MONSTER AND THE JOB SEARCH

FaceBook, LinkedIn, and Monster.com would have you believe that you can have instant contact with untold numbers of potential employers. It's true. True for you and millions of other users of these sites.

It's worth asking yourself: If this is such an effective way to get in touch with potential employers, why are there still 12.5 million unemployed people in the country as of this writing?

---

15   Sutton, Gary. <u>Launch!</u> (pp. 210-213), 2007

> Case in Point:
>
> An associate of mine, Gary Sutton, who in his career was a CEO of seven small businesses and author of <u>Launch!</u>, a book for college seniors just beginning their careers, gives an example of using Monster.com to search for job candidates. "When talking with the Monster sales rep, I learned that they had 63,808,793 (at the time) active resumes on line ... I ran a short ad for a position I wanted to fill. The ad cost $150 and generated a stack of resumes that stood two-and one-half inches on my desk."[15]
>
> A standard ream of paper is 500 single sheets and stands two inches high. That means that Gary's small, local ad generated approximately 625 single sheet resumes, give or take. If your resume was in this pile, what do you think your chances would be of getting an interview?

It's the quality of the contacts that you make, not the quantity that counts.

> *TIP: Use Facebook, LinkedIn and Monster.com as networking and/or researching tools, but don't spend too much time with them. Statistics show that they account for only a small percentage of job placements because the odds there are stacked way, way against you.*

INFORMATION VS. KNOWLEDGE

The data that you collect on the Internet is information, not knowledge. Knowledge occurs when data/information are put into your mental database and, combined with other knowledge from your experience, produces understanding. Data overpowers. Knowledge empowers.

Knowledge that leads to understanding that in turn enables you to take effective action and produce results is what will make you successful in life. Data alone can't do this. Consider data to be like raw ore that must be processed to become something of value.

My point is if you spend too much time on the Internet just gathering data and not spending time in the real world turning data into knowledge and understanding by engaging with other people and real life experiences, your personal and professional harvest will probably be a poor one.

We can become slaves to Facebook, Twitter, Monster, YouTube, name-your-robot, and in the process lose a lot of time. Whoever, in the distant past before the Internet was even a preposterous dream, said "Time Is Money," knew what they were talking about. Get the hell off the Internet and go out and make some money *doing* something, *making* something. "But I'll make money on the Internet," you say, "and become a millionaire." OK, maybe you're the one or two or three in a million, like Bill Gates, or Steve Jobs, or Mark Zuckerberg, but the odds are astronomical against that happening. Get out into the world and make some great money. You've earned your shot at it.

USEFUL JOB SEARCH INTERNET SITES

CareerBuilder	Careerjet
Indeejigsaw.com	jobhunt.org
LinkedIn	Monster
myJoblinx	spoke.com
vault.com	wetfeet.com
zoominfo.com	

Add your own resources.

APPENDIX D
THE IMPORTANCE OF GOOD CREDIT IN GETTING THAT GREAT JOB

Your college degree will enable you to *make* twice as much money in your lifetime as a person with a high school diploma. Good credit will help you *keep* it.

The dollar difference between a high school diploma and a bachelor's degree, as of September 2012, is about *one-million dollars* over your working career. According to the US Census Bureau, high school graduates will earn approximately $1.2 million in their working life; people with a bachelor's degree, $2.1 million; a master's degree will get you $2.5 million.[16] You will work hard for that money; why give a large portion of it back because of the higher interest rates you will be subject to if you don't have good credit?

First things first. Establishing good credit is very important before you begin your career. Many companies today check a job candidate's credit scores with the major credit agencies as a matter of course. They do so because they are trying to get as much information about you as they can, including information about your character. In this respect, being accountable for your credit equates to good character. *Id est que est.* ("It is what it is.")

Many companies believe that your credit score is an important indicator of how responsible you are about financial things and by extension how responsible you would be on the job. Since they are about to entrust you with sensitive, proprietary information regarding their business, a good credit score tells them that you will probably treat their information as you would your personal finances.

---

16   US Census Data 2010 20 Aug. 2011 <http://2010.census.gov/2010census/data>

A survey by The Society of Human Resources Management found that 47% of companies conduct credit background checks on some candidates. Thirteen percent conduct checks on all job candidates.[17]

A good credit score is also an indicator of how well you manage important things in your life. You will be managing something at your first or next career employer, whether it's people, projects, customer relations, or things. Would they feel secure in offering you a position based upon your current credit score?

Given its importance not only to your next job interview but also to the next five decades or so of your personal life, you must start establishing good credit as soon as possible, if you haven't already done so, or repairing your credit status if it's not so hot right now.

For the purposes of this book, I'm going to deal with the subject of credit only as it affects your next job interview. There are many good sources of information on credit as a general topic that can be found on the Internet and other sources. It's extremely important to study the overall effects of credit, both good and bad, as they will affect your future. Your proper use of good credit will mean hundreds of thousands of dollars to you over the course of your lifetime by determining what interest rate you will get on your home mortgage, your next car, your credit cards ... anything that requires revolving credit or a monthly payment.

TIP: Let's assume that you have not established a credit history or credit score, for whatever reason. Your best bet is to start small by applying for a gas card, a retail (department store) card or bankcard associated with your checking account. This will be relatively easy to do if you don't have any previous blemishes in whatever credit history you may have.

You can see if there is any credit history on you by applying for a free credit report from one of the three major credit rating agencies. You're entitled to one free report every calendar year. Claim your free copy at www.annual creditreport.com. (This is the only authorized source for free credit reports.)

Once you have established credit, you have to build on it and protect it. You must manage it constantly as one of the primary duties of your personal CEO status.

---

17   "Law barring credit checks could aid jobless." <u>Sacramento Bee</u> 13 Oct. 2011.

An article by Ester Pak (an assistant site editor at Morningstar), from <u>The Short Answer</u>, defines the basis for determining your credit score: "FICO scores (named after Fair-Isaac Corporation, the company that developed the methods for calculating the scores) are the most commonly used scores by lenders as they attempt to gauge a borrower's risk and reliability."[18]

Your FICO score actually comprises three scores, one from each of the credit bureaus: TransUnion, Equifax, and Experian. Each score from the individual agencies runs from 300 (very bad) to 850 (exceptionally good). *The higher the score, the lower your risk.*

You build on your credit score by paying your bills *on time.* Paying on time accounts for 35% of your credit score. Your total debt amount as a percentage of your available credit accounts for 30% of your score, while the length of your credit history accounts for 15%. Any new credit you acquire accounts for 10%, and the types of credit you have, 10%.

From the values above carried by the components of the FICO, it's apparent that paying your bills on time is critical to maintaining a good credit score. Late payments can stay on your credit record for seven years, maybe more. Paying down your debt, even if it just a little each month, is also extremely important.

It will take a while to build up a good credit history, at least two years. Begin now to get your FICO in the 650 to 700 range as soon as possible. Later, make sure it stays above 750.

"*Now* you tell me how important all this credit stuff is!!!" you say. If that's your view, it probably means that you have made a mistake or two in your young credit life.

There is a way out of your mess. Ms. Pak states: "If a history of making late payments with a credit card company has adversely affected your score, make it a priority to keep paying your bills on time going forward. [Even though] delinquencies remain on your credit report for seven years ... and rebuilding your credit history might not be fun, it's possible to undo black marks on your record."[19]

---

18   Pak, Ester. "How to Keep a Credit Score High." 26 July 2011. <u>The Short Answer</u> <http://morningstar.com>

19   Ibid.

It's part of the price you pay for being your own CEO, for getting the job you want, and for keeping a lot of that money you are about to make.

As of this writing, a new California law, Assembly Bill 22 has changed the rules of the game when it comes to using credit scores in the elimination process of potential job applicants by barring most employers from using credit checks to evaluate job candidates. Most states don't have such laws as yet, but California is the seventh state that does.[20]

The catch here is that the new law doesn't apply to all candidates. As in most things legal, the devil is in the details: Positions excluded from the law are law enforcement, Department of Justice, and most managerial positions, especially those that control $10,000 or more during their workday. Background checks of job candidates for the above positions may still be conducted.

Bottom line: It's still fairly easy for employers to check for significant flaws in your background, including bad credit. Make it a priority to make yours an asset, not a liability.

---

20   "Law barring credit checks could aid jobless." Sacramento Bee 13 Oct. 2011.

APPENDIX E
STUDENT QUESTION FORUM AND JOB FAIR SURVEY

STUDENT QUESTION FORUM

During some of my recent seminars at Sonoma State University, I asked students at the conclusion if they would like to participate in a questionnaire about the seminar and about the job search in general. Participation in the questionnaire was entirely voluntary and anonymous.

JOB SEMINAR QUESTIONNAIRE/2012

(Prepared by Kenneth A. Heinzel, MS)

1. What <u>concerns you most</u> about interviewing for a job?

2. What <u>resources have you used</u> so far in researching how to interview for a job?

3. If you had <u>one question to ask an expert</u> about an upcoming job interview, what would it be?

4. What would be <u>most useful</u> for you, as a college student, in <u>a job interview book</u>?

5a. What has been <u>most useful</u> to you in this job interview seminar?

5b. What would you want to <u>learn more about</u>?

6. Any other questions, comments, or thoughts?

This questionnaire is for research purposes, data collection and illustration in the development of the job interview seminar and written materials. May I have your consent to use your responses? Only your first name and initial would be used.

Signed: _____ Date _____

The students' responses revealed a broad array of observations and deeply-felt concerns. By far, the four greatest concerns of student job interviewees were:

1. **Stress and stress management.** Closely related concerns were: fear of failure in the interview; nervousness; not answering questions properly; committing a gaffe (i.e., "looking like a dummy").

2. **Questions**... specifically, those asked by the interviewer, and how to prepare answers for them. Also, what questions should students/candidates ask of the interviewer.

3. **Beating the competition**. How do I stand out?

4. **First impressions.** What are they expecting?

I've provided a short answer for each of the four top Forum questions below, followed by a chapter reference where you will find a more complete answer.

Stress and Stress Management

Q: *How can I get over my fear of failure in the interview?* (Derek S.)

Short Answer: If you are properly prepared and have gone through your calmness routine, you will do fine. See also: "What if you're waiting for the interview and you get nervous" (Ch. 8).

Q: *Can you give me some stress management tips?* (Adam G.)

Short Answer: Ask an experienced person in your support group what they do to relieve stress before the interview. Review stress-relieving techniques such as deep breathing and visualization. See also: "Your Support Group" (Ch. 2) and, "What if you're waiting for the interview and you get nervous" (Ch. 8).

Q: *What's the best way to overcome my nerves before interviewing?* (Dave T.)

Short Answer: Go to your quiet place within and visualize a place, experience or thought that is calming for you. See also: "What if you're naturally shy" (Ch. 8).

Q: *How do you respond to a question that you are truly stumped on?* (Christine A.)

<u>Short Answer</u>: Ensure you understand the question to begin with; if not, calmly ask the interviewer to repeat or rephrase question so you understand it — this will also give you more time to think. Then give the best answer you can. See also: "The Importance of Rehearsing" (Ch. 3).

Q: *My biggest concern is being rejected.* (Alyssa M.)

<u>Short Answer</u>: Sometimes rejection is not a bad thing; the job may not have been a fit for you and there will be other opportunities. Use every interview as a learning opportunity about yourself and what you are looking for. Go to a trusted friend in your support group and explain why you feel this way. Ask them what they have done to get over rejection in the past. See also: "Your Support Group" (Ch. 2).

Q: *What's the worst thing you could say to blow your chances of obtaining the position?* (Dion A.)

<u>Short Answer</u>: There is no "one worst thing" you could say. There are several. Many involve not being prepared or properly rehearsed ... or not telling the truth. See also: "Final Prep Checklist /Interviewing Action Plan" (Ch. 3).

Q: *What are some common mistakes that interviewees make?* (Anthony C.; Krista S.)

<u>Short Answer</u>: Not having researched the company well enough before the interview is a very common one; also, being late to the interview, not dressing professionally, asking about salary or the company's vacation policy right off the bat. See also: "The Interviewer's Point of View" (Ch. 3).

Questions Asked by the Interviewer

Q: *What questions should I focus on that the interviewer might ask?* (Brian S.)

<u>Short Answer</u>: Who are you? (Tell me about yourself.) Also, why you believe you are the best-qualified candidate for the job. See also: "The Basic Four Questions" (Ch. 5).

Q: *What are behavioral questions in the interview?* (Kersti O.)

<u>Short Answer</u>: These are questions related to results you have produced in the past, in order that the interviewer can project what you might do for them in the future. The concept behind this is that past behavior is an indicator

of future performance. See also: "Other Interview Questions You Might Be Asked" (Ch. 5).

Q: *What do I do if I'm surprised by a question?* (Heather S.)

Short Answer: Expect to be surprised by a question at some point in the interview. The interviewer wants to see how you handle being surprised. Learning to think on your feet is the important lesson here. It's important to relax, take a few moments to think of the answer before you respond. Mock interviews can help a lot to develop poise. See also: "Mock Interviews" and "The Importance of Rehearsing" (Ch. 3).

Q: *What's the best way to answer questions about my weaknesses and strengths?* (Tonia D.)

Short Answer: Answer questions about your weaknesses in a positive way. For example, we all have simple weaknesses, such as falling behind in our reading because of time spent on volunteer activities. Explaining this turns a small negative into a positive. Never say anything negative about anything. Answer questions about your strengths with examples of positive results you have achieved in the past. For example, "As a leader of a team during an internship with a large retailer last summer, I was able to get people to complete their tasks on time and produce positive results." See also: "Soft Skills" (Ch. 3) and "Always Be Positive" (Ch. 7).

Q: *How do I say "I don't know" to a question asked by an interviewer?* (James H.)

Short Answer: Say, "I don't know, but may I have a moment to consider it?" See also: "The Importance of Rehearsing" (Ch. 3).

Q: *How do you answer unexpected questions?* (Anonymous)

Short Answer: There are always unexpected questions in the interview — *always* — and there are potentially dozens and dozens of them. You will never know what these questions will be in advance. The best path to take is to learn to think on your feet so that you can respond intelligently to any question. See also: "Mock Interviews" (Ch. 3).

Questions Asked by the Interviewee

Q: *What questions should I be sure to ask the interviewer?* (Rob S.; Matt P.)

<u>Short Answer</u>: There are several. One might be, "You obviously like working for your company; would you please tell me why?" See also: "Questions to Ask the Interviewer" (Ch. 5).

Q: *What questions should I ask at the end of the interview?* (Kersti O.)

<u>Short Answer</u>: "If you were to hire me, what's the most important thing I could do for you in the first 90 days on the job?" See also: "Questions to Ask the Interviewer" (Ch. 5).

Beating the Competition and Standing Out

Q: *How do I blow out my competition?* (Cline B.)

<u>Short Answer</u>: There are several things you must do. One is to be sure that you have thoroughly researched the company. Don't go to the interview unless you have done this. See also: "The Interviewer's Point of View" (Ch. 3).

Q: *How can I stand out in a good way?* (Carrin L.)

<u>Short Answer</u>: Know the importance of a good attitude and be sure to bring it to the interview. See also: "The Key Element of the Job Search" (Ch. 1).

Q: *How can I make myself stand out if I don't have an outstanding back-ground?* (Maura B.)

<u>Short Answer</u>: There are several things you can do. One is to have questions prepared to ask the interviewer that relate to the specific job in question. See also: "Questions to Ask the Interviewer" (Ch. 5).

Q: *If I feel that I am under-qualified, how do I handle that?* (Max L.)

<u>Short Answer</u>: Construct a new Personal Value Proposition (see Ch. 4). Doing this is key to convincing the interviewer that you can do the job. See also: "Selling Techniques" (Ch. 4).

Q: *If I could perfect one thing about me in the interview, what would that be?* (K.M.)

<u>Short Answer</u>: Summarize your Personal Value Proposition (Ch. 4) that explains your strengths in terms of specific benefits to the interviewer. See also: "You Are a Real Salesperson, Too" (Ch. 4).

Q: *What's the most important thing that the interviewer is looking for?* (Lauren S.)

<u>Short Answer</u>: The interviewer is looking for someone who can do the job *and* provide "yes" answers to the hidden interview questions. Soft skills, such as good communication, good energy and enthusiasm are also high on the interviewer's agenda. See also: *The Hidden Interview* under "What Can You Do For Me?" (Ch. 5).

Q: *If I have no job experience what can I say to help me look good?* (Anonymous)

<u>Short Answer</u>: You must be able to show that you have produced results in the past at any important endeavor you undertook, even if you didn't earn any money doing it. See also: "Your Personal Value Proposition" (Ch. 4).

Q: *What is it that sets you apart from everyone else?* (Taylor E.)

<u>Short Answer</u>: Results you have achieved in the past that can relate directly to the job in question. Eagerness to learn, enthusiasm, and a positive attitude are all important, too. See also: *Strengths & Benefits* under "You are a Real Salesperson, Too" (Ch. 4).

First Impressions

Q: *What's the best way to give a great first impression and hold their attention?* (Ria L.)

<u>Short Answer</u>: Dress properly. Don't decide this alone; get advice from your support group. Non-verbals are important, too, including eye contact, a firm handshake, proper posture when sitting. See also: "The Importance of First Impressions" (Ch. 3).

Q: *Do interviewers really make up their minds in the first 10 minutes of the interview?* (Joelle E.)

<u>Short Answer</u>: Interviewers form an impression of what they think about you early in the interview, but usually won't make a final decision at that point unless you did or said something awful. They will make a final decision about you as a serious candidate sometime within the next hour after they have gathered more information. Still, immediate impressions are very important. See also: "The Importance of First Impressions" (Ch. 3).

Q: *What's the best way to make a connection with the interviewer?* (Angela C.)

<u>Short Answer</u>: Bring a positive attitude and establish good chemistry early in the interview. See also: "The Key Element of the Job Search" (Ch. 1) and "Chemistry" (Ch. 4).

Q: *What are some examples of "ice-breaking" methods in the interview?* (B.P.S.)

<u>Short Answer</u>: You must engage in "small talk" to start things off, maybe something related to the company that you have read, the architecture in the lobby, pictures you see in the interviewing room, something that connects you naturally (even talking about the weather!) See also: "Final Prep Checklist/Interviewing Action Plan" (Ch. 3) and "The Initial Interview with Management" (Ch. 4).

Q: *What's the best way to make the interviewer comfortable with me?* (Nick B.)

<u>Short Answer</u>: Be cordial, have a positive attitude, start off by thanking the interviewer for seeing you, and say something positive about their company. Have a good 2-Minute bio ready. See also: "Who Are You?" (Ch. 5).

Q: *What are some of the common things that the interviewer is looking for?* (Courtney G.)

<u>Short Answer</u>: What kind of energy are you putting out? Will you fit into the company culture? See also: "Job Fair Survey" (Appendix E) and "Soft Skills" (Ch. 3).

Q: *How can I come across as being more friendly?* (Jennilyn B.)

<u>Short Answer</u>: Don't be a phony. Bring your best energy. Be courteous. Express a genuine interest in the company. See also: "Chemistry" (Ch. 4).

How do you know if you are prepared for the interview?

Q: *Is there a way of knowing which questions to prepare for?* (Jesus V.)

<u>Short Answer</u>: You will never know in advance the specific questions that an interviewer will ask. However, the Basic Four Questions are always asked

in some form during every interview (Ch. 5). Having answers prepared for these will give you a big edge. See also: "Other Interview Questions You Might be Asked" (Ch. 5).

Q: *How can I put together a practice interview and make it realistic?* (A. P.)

Short Answer: Ask a member of your personal support group to put you through some tough questions that they make up. An experienced friend in business can do this. See also: "Mock Interviews" (Ch. 3).

Q: *What's the best way to prepare for an interview for a job that you don't want but really need?* (Jessica E. W.)

Short Answer: The only way to interview for a job — any job — is to go in full force as if this is the only job on the planet for you right now. Faking enthusiasm, acting, or appearing to be desperate are interview killers. See also: "The Key Element of the Job Search" (Ch. 1).

Q: *How will I know when I'm really prepared for the interview?* (Ethan C.)

Short Answer: Have you researched the company enough that you could write a short paper about them? Do you have at least six or seven questions prepared to ask them? See also: "The Basic Reason Why Companies Want to Hire You" (Ch. 3).

Q: *Do you have a checklist on what to prepare for in the interview?* (Taylor M.)

Short Answer: Read all of Chapter 3.

Q: *Do you have a checklist of what <u>not</u> to do in the interview?* (Jennifer F.)

Short Answer: The big ones on the checklist are: *Don't* come unprepared or without questions, dressed inappropriately or with a bad attitude. There are dozens of things you shouldn't do and many of them are specific to you. Read this book and then re-read it. At that point, create your own checklist.

The Interview Going Bad and Body Language

Q: *What are the signs of the interview going south, and what can I do about it?* (Teal J.)

<u>Short Answer</u>: There are several. Among them, miscommunication of any kind, and negative body language exhibited by the interviewer. See also: "What if things start to go bad in the interview?" (Ch. 8).

Q: *When do you know that the interviewer is not interested in you, or not going to hire you?* (Anonymous)

<u>Short Answer</u>: If the interviewer starts wrapping things up in 15-20 minutes, you're in trouble. See also: "Your 30-Day Plan" (Ch. 4).

Q: *What's the best way to understand body language?* (Teal J.)

<u>Short Answer</u>: Study it as you would any new language you were trying to learn. Go to Google and YouTube for some excellent videos that show examples of body language.

Q: *What are the keys to turning around a negative interview?* (Kyle S.)

<u>Short Answer</u>: When things have obviously gone bad, take charge and ask the interviewer if you can re-visit a question they just asked to clarify what you said. Also, have something dramatic to show them. See also: "Your 30-Day Plan" (Ch. 4).

Networking

Q: *Can you give me an example of how to get an interview, when I couldn't otherwise get one?* (Meagan D.)

<u>Short Answer</u>: Your best resource for getting an interview is your own personal network, which has your support group at its core. At least 70% of job leads come from this source. See also: "Networking and Your Support Group" (Ch. 2).

Q: *What resources can I use to make company contacts through others?* (Anonymous)

<u>Short Answer</u>: All of this is covered in Chapter 2.

Q: *How do I create a network so it's not awkward to contact someone whom I talked to only a few times?* (Arianna V-B)

<u>Short Answer</u>: Give them something they might be interested in or need. Networking isn't just about seeking help; it's also about giving it. See also: "Your Support Group" (Ch. 2).

Personal Strengths Explained As Benefits to the Company

Q: *Can you explain how my attributes (strengths) can be explained as benefits to the company to help them make money?* (Anonymous)

<u>Short Answer</u>: You have to sell the interviewer as to why you are the solution to their problems. Your personal value proposition is the place to start. See also: *Personal Value Proposition* under "Selling Techniques" (Ch. 4).

Lack of Experience

Q: *How do I present myself so that my age or lack of experience won't hinder me?* (Meagan D.)

<u>Short Answer</u>: Even if you have had no direct job experience yet, you still have accomplished things in the past that produced results of some kind. These results are your best strengths, which must be expressed in terms of benefits to the interviewer and their company. See also: "How to Become an Effective Salesperson … of You" (Ch. 4).

Q: *How should I describe my experience and myself in a professional way even if I do not have a lot of experience?* (Joelle E.)

<u>Short Answer</u>: Be well rehearsed and knowledgeable about your personal strengths. Tell the interviewer how these strengths will solve their problems as far as this job is concerned. See also: "The Basic Reason Why Companies Want to Hire You" (Ch. 3).

Miscellaneous

Q: *What's the most memorable thing I can do or say in the interview?* (Jessica M.)

<u>Short Answer</u>: There are several; for example, "I can help you reach your goals and here's how." (At this point offer specifics that are unique to you that will get the job done). See also: "What Can You Do For Me?" (Ch. 5).

Q: *What's the number one thing that the interviewer is looking for?* (Michael R.)

<u>Short Answer</u>: I wish it were that simple. It isn't. Other than "Can this person do the job?", the interviewer is looking for a number of key things, such as soft skills. See also: "Company Culture" (Ch. 4).

Q: *What's the most important thing to remember while being interviewed?* (Katie O.)

<u>Short Answer</u>: The most important thing to remember during the interview is to be yourself. No acting or faking allowed. You're well prepared, well rehearsed, have high energy, and have good questions to ask. Now, go sell yourself in terms of what the interviewer is looking for, as described in the job description. See also: "Characteristics of a Successful Salesperson" (Ch. 4).

Q: *What do you cover in a bio about yourself?* (Stacey B.)

<u>Short Answer</u>: Explain who you are at this moment in your life. Suggested topics: why you chose your major; what are some of your values; where you are from; describe your family; where you see yourself in five years. Use your creativity. See also: "Who Are You?/Your 2-Minute Bio" (Ch. 5).

Q: *How do I get an interview for a job that uses a recruiter, and I don't have access to them?* (Anonymous)

<u>Short Answer</u>: Go directly to the hiring manager, or any manager who was referred to you by a friend. If you can't get to the hiring manager, don't submit your resume to the company HR department. Most recruiters involved will not help you at that point because the company will not pay a fee for someone who is already in their database. But if you can get the recruiter's name, then call the recruiter directly. See also: "Recruiters & Other Professional Helpers" (Ch. 2).

Q: *What should I do after each interview with the same company, i.e., 1st, 2nd, 3rd, 4th?* (Angela C.)

<u>Short Answer</u>: After every management interview, if you get a definite, specific next step to take from the interviewer, follow that. After every interview with the same company, send a short personal note, if time between interviews allows, plus an e-mail. See also: "Sending Notes and Other Follow Up" (Ch. 6).

Q: *What's the one piece of advice that you know now that you wish you would have known before the interview?* (Alex S.)

Short Answer: Train yourself to be as relaxed as you can be, and be yourself. See also: "The Importance of Happiness" (Ch. 1).

Q: *What is the interviewer looking for besides the basic requirements of the job?* (Alex S.)

Short Answer: In addition to basic skills, they are looking for soft skills, such as the ability to communicate well. You must be aware of these skills because they are critical to beating your competition See also: "Soft Skills" (Ch. 3) and "Chemistry" (Ch. 4).

Q: *Do you have a timeline of what to do from the first interview to the job offer?* (Amanda S.)

Short Answer: In addition to the notes and e-mails you will send, keep doing research on the company for any "new" information you could bring up in your next meeting. This is an excellent way to show the interviewer that you are very interested in the company. See also: "Sending Notes & Other Follow Up" (Ch. 6).

Other Questions

Q: *How can I demonstrate to the interviewer that hiring me will add to their bottom line?*

Short Answer: Results, results, results. Give examples of anything *signifi-cant* that you have achieved in the past, even if you were not paid for it. See also: "Why Should I Hire You?" and "What Can You Do For Me?" (Ch. 5).

Q: *What's the most important thing that you can control in the interview?*

Short Answer: Your attitude. Attitude is also one of the few things you have complete control over in your life. See also: "The Key Element of the Job Search" (Ch. 1).

Q: *Why is it important to ask for the job at the end of the interview?*

Short Answer: The interviewer expects you to. And you will hurt your chances of moving to the next round or getting an offer if you don't. See also: "Selling Techniques" (Ch. 4).

Q: *How will I know that I'm really prepared for the interview?*

<u>Short Answer</u>: You will know when you feel that you are ready to take your final exam — the interview itself. If you haven't prepared well, you will know in your gut that you're not ready. If you don't have several well-thought-out questions, you're not ready. If you haven't rehearsed and done at least one mock interview, you probably won't do well. See also: "Final Prep Checklist/ Interviewing Action Plan" (Ch.3).

Q: *What's the best way to sell myself?*

<u>Short Answer</u>: Read Chapter 5.

Q: *Do the same rules of interviewing apply to non-profits and social enterprises as they do in the for-profit world?*

<u>Short Answer</u>: The basic rules of interviewing always apply in any interview. However, there are some significant differences in procedure and character in non-profit and social enterprise interviews. See also: "What if it's a committee interview?" (Ch. 8) and "The Non-Profit World and Money" (Ch. 3).

Q: *What do I say when the interviewer asks, "Convince me that you can do this job"?*

<u>Short Answer</u>: If this question is asked at the end of the interview, summarize all the positive things that you spoke about during the interview, particularly results you achieved in the past, and *close 'em!* If this question is asked at the beginning of the interview, give an example of something you did in the past that produced results that relates specifically to the job you're interviewing for.

Q: *How do I deal with what the interviewer may be looking for other than job-specific skills?*

<u>Short Answer</u>: This goes beyond the basic job description and seeks information about what the interviewer is looking for related to the "soft skills" of the candidate, such as the ability to get along with co-workers. See also: "Chemistry" and "Company Culture" (Ch. 4).

JOB FAIR SURVEY

In March 2012 I went to a Campus Job Fair at Sonoma State that brought together approximately 50 companies as well as representatives of the Armed Services.

My objective was to get first-hand information from interviewers and company recruiters about what they look for in today's college student/recent grad job candidates. While the sample of companies in the survey was small, the respondents provided valuable insight from an interviewer's point of view. And, significantly, what interviewers and recruiters said they want in candidates was the same, *across the board.*

Companies/entities participating in my survey:

Calix	**Nelson Personnel**
Fireman's Fund Insurance	**Northwestern Mutual**
G.C. Micro	**Target**
Hertz	**United States Army**
Kohl's	**Vector Marketing**

Questions and Responses

Question 1: What are some of the important things that you look for in today's student job candidates?

Responses:

- **Are they prepared for the interview?** *(Every company mentioned this.)* Do they have knowledge of about our company? Have they done their research? Do they have prepared questions?

- Do they communicate well?

- Are they enthusiastic about interviewing with us?

- Do they have leadership qualities?

- Can they work independently (possess critical thinking skills and still have the ability to collaborate)?

- Do they show some kind of passion about their field of study, or about what they do?

- What are they most proud of, and how well do they sell themselves?

- Are they personable, with good eye contact and body language?

- Do they have experience in their field, especially internships?

- Are they a culture fit?

- Do they have a GPA of 3.0+?

Question 2: If you had one piece of advice to give to a candidate, what would that be?

Responses:

- **Come prepared!**

- Network with recent grads.

- Have a good attitude and show confidence.

- Do your best to connect with the interviewer (establish chemistry).

- Be prepared to explain why you want to work with this company. *(This is a make it or break it issue with most companies.)*

- Dress well, not sloppily.

- Listen before you answer.

Question 3: What are some of the things that turn you off to a student candidate?

Responses:

- **Not being prepared**.

- Not having questions, especially at the end of the interview.

- Lack of confidence.

- Not being really present in the interview.

- Bad body language.

- Appearing to be uncoachable (being way over-confident or cocky)

Question 4: Do you have any other observations or impressions of today's student candidates?

Responses:

- Respondents said that they expect most candidates to be nervous at the beginning of the interview. *Most mentioned that they would do their best to put the candidate at ease by starting with casual conversation (small talk); giving them a preview of what's to come in the interview; stating that they realize that the candidate is new to the interview process and try to calm them down. One interviewer's policy is to send an e-mail in advance to give the candidate a general idea of what to expect in the interview.*

- Some interviewers mentioned that today's candidates don't seem to be as disciplined as candidates in the past.

- Some mentioned that there is a sense of "entitlement" exhibited by some candidates.

- A few mentioned that there is a sense of desperation in some candidates, that they just want a job, any job.

We shall not cease from exploration

And the end of all our exploring

Will be to arrive where we started

And know the place for the first time.

(T.S. Eliot, "The Four Quartets")

CPSIA information can be obtained at www.ICGtesting.com
Printed in the USA
LVOW11s2141070914

402929LV00001B/139/P